BORN TO FIGHT

BORN TO FIGHT

MARK HUNT
AND BEN MCKELVEY

sphere

SPHERE

First published by Hachette Australia in 2015
This edition published in 2017 by Sphere

1 3 5 7 9 10 8 6 4 2

ISBN 978-0-7515-7029-8

Cover design by Christabelle Designs
Front cover image courtesy of Ryan Loco – ryanloco.com
Back cover images courtesy of Lucy Tui and Getty Images
Typeset in Sabon LT Pro by Bookhouse, Sydney
Printed and bound in Great Britain by
Clays Ltd, St Ives plc

Papers used by Sphere are from well-managed forests
and other responsible sources.

MIX
Paper from
responsible sources
FSC® C104740

Sphere
An imprint of
Little, Brown Book Group
Carmelite House
50 Victoria Embankment
London EC4Y 0DZ

An Hachette UK Company
www.hachette.co.uk

www.littlebrown.co.uk

For Jesus Christ, my lord and saviour; my wife, Julie;
the people who have helped me to be where I am;
and all those in the struggle.

M.H.

Thanks go to Mark, Victoria and Julie for their honesty,
and to Val, Val, Laura and Luce for their love.

B.M.

Preface

ARENA CIUDAD DE MÉXICO
MEXICO CITY, MEXICO
2014

I could tell Fabrício Werdum was about to put his hands up just a bit too high. There was going to be a little moment when his gloves would be in front of his eyes, and not on me. I knew it. I felt it.

Just a moment, that's all I needed.

There it went.

I leapt across the four or so metres between us, leading with a little, confusing jab, then a loaded-up overhand right.

BAM.

Caught him right above the ear. Down he went like a big old bag of Brazilian bananas.

He's a big bloke, Werdum – tall and experienced. Some people were saying I wouldn't be able to hit him. I was too short, and Fab was too good. I didn't have enough notice to get fit, and get fists on him. I was too old, and too fat. Blah blah blah.

I knew I could get him. There's no man in the world I can't hit. If you've only got two arms and two legs, I can get to you. That's a talent, given to me by God himself.

My fists have taken me around the world. People have filled stadiums to see these fists in action. Men have feared them – professional fighters, gangsters and criminals and, I'm sorry to say, some poor people who stumbled along the wrong street on the wrong day. Now a fist of mine had put Fabrício Werdum on his bum. Fab wasn't finished yet, but I could see the UFC Heavyweight Interim title right there, on the edge of his jaw.

There were 20,000 fight fans inside the arena hooting and hollering, and a shitload more watching on TV, especially in New Zealand and Australia, my two homes. They were cheering for me. I could hear them, and I could feel them.

Me? I felt nothing. I was empty.

People assumed later it was the altitude and the cut – 2250 metres above sea level, and twenty kilograms shed in three and a half weeks – that had brought on my malaise. I really hated being hungry, but that wasn't it.

It was something else.

I was forty years old and had lived five lives, four of them violent. This was just another bloke sprawled on the ground after I'd given him the skin of my knuckles. This was just another pair of unfocused eyes, just another man on the ground below me, with his hand up, and his chin down.

I was thinking about my wife, Julie, and my little ones. I was just an inch away from another world title, just a second, but I was thinking about the quietness of home, the kids' toys and the food in my fridge.

This fight was just another moment to get through. Winning this fight wouldn't be the best thing that would happen to me in this life. Losing certainly wouldn't be the worst.

I've been beaten, tortured and jailed. I've lived as a bad man and a good man. I've been addicted, homeless and broke. I've been lost, and found. This life would have ruined many, but God, he gave me the gifts I needed to keep going.

Those gifts were at the end of my arms.

Woe to the man who's given a gift by God but ignores it. Woe to him.

I walked back a few steps, bunched my fists and let Werdum stand back up again.

Come on then, get your ass over here. Let's see what you got. Gummon, boy.

Gummon.

Chapter 1

SOUTH AUCKLAND, NEW ZEALAND
1974

> Mark was still a baby when all hell broke loose. He'd be black
> and blue head-to-toe regularly. I'd have to wash away the blood,
> massage his bruises and put salt on his wounds, so Dad could
> give him another beating. At about five Mark started to become
> a thief, and a violent maniac, but how would he know any
> better? He didn't even understand what love was until he met
> Julie. There were good parts of him but, that survived during
> the abuse, and those parts became the soul of my brother.
>
> **VICTORIA NAND (SISTER)**

The last time I saw the darkness was on the day my dad died.

The first time I saw that thing I didn't know what it was. I was terrified of it, though, like nothing I've been scared of before or since. The last time I saw it, I finally knew what it was. I knew who it was. It was the devil, come to take my old man away.

I first saw that darkness in South Auckland at the wheel of a totalled car I'd recently stolen. I'd come round a corner just a little too fast, bounced off the kerb and up into a light pole. When I woke up, my partner-in-crime, Bronson, was pulling me out of the wreckage, but there was something wrong about the night – it was as though the contrast of the sky was all jacked up, and there was a burning smell.

As I ran, I saw a giant claw coming down through the clouds, reaching towards me. I felt myself disappearing from my body, and started to run in third person, as though I was a character from *Grand Theft Auto*.

I was scared that night – one of the few instances I ever was. Bronson and I ran like I don't think either of us ever have since. Bronson saw it too. He was never quite the same dude afterwards.

I saw the darkness in Sydney once, too, when I was half-conscious in a flophouse in Surry Hills, surrounded by junkies and prostitutes and recently but deeply addicted. That day it didn't come fully formed, but as something nebulous. I still recognised it, though, the moment it appeared, with that smell and that feeling.

I asked what that thing wanted this time – I was in a bold mood – but it had nothing to say. It just surveyed my surroundings of shit, before leaving, with its faint smell of acidity and ash lingering.

Those two times I think the devil was just visiting, or perhaps leaving a warning. The last time I saw it, though, it came complete – fully raised, fully formed, and here to do its work.

A few months before my dad died, his eyes had started to go and his skin was turning green. When he finally went to hospital, he was diagnosed with late-stage pancreatic cancer. None of us kids knew why the old man ignored the doctors and refused their help, but none of us were surprised either. After his diagnosis, the old bastard discharged himself, walked the many kilometres home and slumped on the couch. There he stayed, taking no medication and no visitors, instead just rotting away like meat left in the sun.

A few months after his diagnosis, it was time for me to throw the shadow of Charles Sale Hunt over my shoulder, toss him into the car and drive him to the hospital to die. On the old man's last day alive, I pushed my wheelchair-bound mum, who'd been made immobile and silent by multiple strokes, into a giant, bright, sparse, white-tiled hospital room where he was laid out on a bed. Almost all the life had gone from my father; his face was sunken, with yellow eyes like the Hulk's. His hair was white and stringy, and his once strong body had wasted away.

What was left in him was about to be taken by the giant that stood next to his bed, which was dark like a void, hooded, huge, familiar and with a stench that was over-powering. I could feel the immense, crackling, untethered power of that figure, but I dared not look directly at it. I could feel that even looking at that thing could level buildings, maybe even cities.

I kept my eyes on my father. As I stared at the old man, I knew he was going with the devil that day. I also knew there was nothing to be done about it. My father had lived his life, made his choices and committed his sins. Now he was going with the darkness.

So be it.

I find it hard to remember my parents' faces these days. I always remember my dad's blue overalls and the blue overcoat he wore in winter, and I remember my mum's big old Afro. Sometimes, though, in my memories, smudges have replaced their faces.

I'm assuming my parents' story was similar to the rest of the FOB (fresh off the boat) Islanders in New Zealand at the time. The Samoan economy was pretty basic, so if you didn't want to work in the fields like your parents and grandparents before you, you probably wanted to think about hopping over to New Zealand.

My parents had both been married before they met each other, so maybe that helped push them west. I don't know that for sure, though. I don't know much about my parents' history, and almost nothing about their parents and beyond. What I do know is that in 1965 Charles Sale Hunt and his wife, Meleiota, moved from Savai'i in Samoa to Auckland, and by 1974, when I was dropped into this world at St Heliers Hospital, pretty much all they had to show for themselves was Victoria, five years older than me; Steve, three years older; John, two years older; and now me, the baby.

My first ever memories were just feelings, and there was one feeling that I remember more than the rest: hunger. Dad had a job at the beginning, a manufacturing gig at the Kent Heating factory, but he could never put enough food on the table. Couldn't, wouldn't, whatever.

My memories of places and people started to form when we four kids were shipped off from our one-bedroom place in the Auckland suburb of Mount Eden to Savai'i to live with my dad's brother and his wife when I was maybe four or five.

Not many people know much about Samoa, which is fair enough; it's a pretty small place – big people, but a small place. Samoa is made up of a series of islands, which lie about 3000 kilometres northeast of New Zealand.

The place looks like you'd expect a Pacific island to look – blue seas, green hills and yellow sand – populated by 200,000 or so locals. There are about the same number of Samoans living in Australia and New Zealand, with the bulk living in New Zealand. Samoa was administrated by New Zealand up until the sixties, so there was an easy immigration path between the two countries.

I don't really know why Mum and Dad sent us over to Samoa. I guess they wanted to give us a better life than the one we were having in Auckland, but I do remember having to catch and cook bats in the fields to eat. So perhaps it wasn't for our benefit.

In Samoa, I remember a house above a shop. I remember a rock pool where my brothers and I once thought we were about to drown. I remember a cousin pulling each of us out of that water by our hair. I remember a picture theatre, which I now realise was probably little more than a darkened room and a projector. I remember stealing biscuits.

I don't recall many of the people in Samoa, but I do remember a little Asian bloke with a badass look on his face, shirt off, black pants, howling like a cat.

WAAAAAATAAAAAAAAH.

Some people were trying to attack this little shirtless guy, but he was fending them off as easily as you might a litter of kittens, his fists and feet flying around like he was a banshee. I don't remember what Uncle and Auntie looked like – they are just smudges now too – but I remember Bruce Lee. That little dude was made out of magic. I loved Bruce Lee and David Carradine, and later Van Damme, Seagal and Norris. There wasn't a problem they couldn't fix.

In Samoa I remember meeting up with my sister, Victoria, once a week in church. That was the only time we'd see her, as tradition dictated that the boys lived with Uncle, and Victoria with Auntie, in a different house. Victoria had been sad in Auckland, and when I saw her at church in Samoa, I noticed she had that same sadness. I didn't figure out why until I was a lot older.

After a year or so we were called back to New Zealand to live with Mum and Dad, this time in a four-bedroom house in Papatoetoe in South Auckland. It may sound like my parents had gotten their shit together, but they hadn't. The house was bigger than what we were living in before, no doubt, but there wasn't really any more food, and now there was debt – debt that fuelled the fire of Dad's anger. Even as a little tacker, I could recognise that.

As soon as we got into that house, the arguments with the neighbours started. Later on I realised that our family, and our house, had a reputation. Mum was loud, but Dad was physical, very physical. We were isolated on our street, and weren't even allowed to talk to the other little Samoan kids next door. Victoria used to pass notes to them asking what life was like in their house, but that act of sedition had to be carried out carefully, because if she was caught, she was getting a beating.

Most of the neighbours didn't like our parents, and they particularly gave Dad a very wide berth. We kids didn't have that luxury. I used to spend a lot of time trying to figure out why the beatings happened: why they happened in general, or what the cause of any specific beating might have been. It's only now that I know they didn't really have much to do with us, they were about something else. That something else I hope never to know about.

Dad would beat us for any little thing, and with any implement. Fists, feet, broom handles, sticks, electrical cords, the hose that went from the washing machine to the tap. That last one really sucked, because it was heavy and it hurt like hell when Dad really got it going, but no matter how hard you got beat with it, it never broke.

With that hose, Dad could just whup until he got tired, and he had energy for that work, man. He loved that hose.

He was big on psychological pain, too, my old man. A beating he seemed to particularly enjoy was forcing us onto our knees on the floor in the sitting room, facing out the window at the pear tree, where he'd go and spend time carefully selecting a whupping branch. We'd hope for a new, young branch, or an old one ready to break, but he'd usually end up with something hefty and durable.

Another of his favourites was calling one of us over, and when we got there, throwing all his weight into a thigh punch. You'd fall to the ground with a dead leg and then he had you. You couldn't run, you just had to lie there and wait for him to do whatever he wanted to do to you. Was he going to get the hose? Was he going to get the broom? Were you going to get the boot? Are those his footsteps?

He also used to like making us beat each other, and if ever we cried, he'd jump in with his man fists and feet. All the beatings were worse if we cried. If we cried, the extra strikes were on us. At the end, the blame was usually equally shared. We shouldn't have been so weak.

When I saw the movie *Wolf Creek*, the cruel bastard of a main character Mick Taylor reminded me of my dad. He would have made a good torturer, the old fella. He really put his heart and soul into his sadism.

I used to think Steve got the worst of it, because he was the oldest boy, and the biggest, and the one most likely to know better than to do whatever it was that we little kids shouldn't be doing – that's why he got his head smashed against the walls and doors. Now I suspect it was just because Dad had had more time to resent him.

I used to think Victoria got off relatively lightly. That didn't mean she didn't get beaten; she was in charge of us boys and had to try to keep us clean and in line, and when she didn't manage it (which was pretty much always) she'd get the crap beaten out of her too. Still, I didn't think she had it as bad as me, Steve and John.

We all thought Dad was soft on Victoria. He used to take her into a room with him, but inside we wouldn't hear the crashes and thumps of a beating, nor would there be blood or bruises when she came out. That shit wasn't fair as far as we knew. We thought something odd was happening in that room, but we didn't know that something was heinous and sinful.

We used to dare each other to go in. Thank fuck we never did.

We didn't know shit about shit. When I knew more about what was going on, I realised Victoria by far had the worst of it, but none of us could comprehend any of that at the time.

I try to remember any light, fun moments we shared as kids, but it's hard to find anything. If there were any board games, or holidays, or trips to the movies, or the rugby, or the museum, or anything that parents and little kids do together then I don't remember them. All I remember about that house is a shitload of beatings and what felt like endless days of hunger.

There was usually some food when Mum was around, but later on she had two jobs, which meant she was never there. Dad cooked sometimes, but when he did it'd be a giant pot of lamb flaps, or something like that, and we'd be eating it for weeks, even after it had gone off.

There was food when someone in the family died, and we couldn't wait for that to happen. Unlike a lot of Samoans, we didn't know our extended family, because most of those who lived in New Zealand were on my mother's side, and Dad forbade us, Mum included, from being in contact with them. We would only see them when someone died, and none of them meant anything to us except a bus ride to a big feed when they finally fucked off from this life. Of course we couldn't wait for that to happen.

There was also food when the Mormons came around. They were the only people who ever came round to that shithole. Those guys from the church used to get to tuck into all kinds of good stuff that our parents would get for them – cake, Milo, chips, Coke, biscuits, all the stuff I would literally have dreams about. When they came we'd poke our heads through the door, salivating, looking at these missionaries with eyes of hatred and jealousy.

We had to be silent when those dudes came around. This was to be a perfect house in front of the church people, and we were to be perfect children. Sometimes John couldn't handle that, though. He was the most introverted and introspective of us kids, but if you ever managed to light his fuse, then the explosion would be measured in megatons.

There was more than one occasion when John couldn't help but scream at the missionaries, telling them to fuck off out of the house. When that happened, Dad would feign surprise and gently tell off my brother, with John fully knowing that each soft word would correlate to strikes from a fist or implement as soon as the Mormons left.

John couldn't help himself. We were as hungry as street dogs, so it was torture watching someone eat, and in our house of starvation no less. It was almost as bad as when we'd catch Mum and Dad in the car, eating fast food, before coming inside and reeking of delicious chips.

I know it wasn't the missionaries' fault we were hungry, and there's no way they could've known they were the only people to get a decent feed at our house. I know that now, anyway.

When they'd leave, we'd jump onto whatever they didn't eat like animals on the Serengeti, and more than once an almighty brawl erupted over who would get the lion's share.

We weren't siblings like you and yours might be, we were desperate competitors, every day fighting a zero-sum game.

Like a lot of Polynesian people in South Auckland, we were born Mormons, and while I did become a man of faith later I really only remember the Church of Jesus Christ of Latter-Day Saints as a place where we'd have to sit down for a long time, wearing uncomfortable clothes.

When I became an adult I realised that the Mormon Church didn't do us right. Those people didn't do my sister right. They knew what was going on with my dad and my sister – it was an open secret at the church. Our bishop knew exactly what was going on with Victoria because she went to him and asked for help. All he ever did was tell off anyone who spoke of what was going on, and he certainly didn't try to help.

I didn't think anything of it at the time, but now I find it weird that no one at the church ever tried to do anything about what was happening to my sister. The church should have been better. Someone should have been stronger. They were meant to be leaders and protectors. They were meant to help their flock when the community needed it – they used to bang on about that. My sister needed it.

Everyone around the neighbourhood knew what my dad was doing, but we boys closest to it only knew vaguely that something rotten was going on, and we certainly didn't understand the gravity of it. At seven I was too young to know what was right and what was wrong, and what happened between men and women. I could only sense the wrongness of it, but I couldn't understand or articulate what was really happening.

Any time I was allowed to leave the house I'd feel an electric unburdening, but there was always a lingering pain when Victoria was left behind. I always got out when I had the chance, though. I'd run from that fucking house.

Sometimes I'd run to the school, or the big tree in the sporting ground, where I could see if Dad was coming to get my ass, but my favourite escape was to the Spaceys, cabinet video games found at most local shops in Auckland at that time.

I especially liked the stand-up fighting games, where my character would punch and kick his way further and further into the story, dependent on my skill. Up, down, left, right, button A, button B – you press the buttons at the right time, move the stick at the right time, you could win. It fed a part of my brain that I'd be shovelling money into for the rest of my life.

How did I get the money to play Spaceys? Sometimes I'd steal other kids' money to play; sometimes – and these were the best times – I'd get to play because John had managed to jury-rig a machine to give us endless free credits.

I remember an instance when John had fixed up Kung Fu Master. Man, the joy of not having to worry about a missed button press, or an errant joystick tilt ending the game was something I'll never forget.

There were no mistakes that couldn't be fixed. I could play that game for the rest of my life. Only John didn't see it that way – eventually he got sick of me buzzing around him, pestering for my turn.

He told me to go home, and if I didn't, he was going to beat my ass. That was no idle threat either. He'd done it before, he'd do it again.

I had to go back home, back to Dad and Victoria and the smell of Dettol. I hated the smell of Dettol before I even knew that Dad was using it to wash himself after his sinful acts. I still can't stand the smell of it now.

Dad was abusing Victoria pretty much from when I was born, so I guess I knew about incest before I knew about sex. It was happening when we were first in New Zealand, it was happening in Samoa – with Dad's brother taking over that fucked-up duty – and it was happening when we came back.

It was always happening and everyone knew. Mum knew, but she'd just laugh about it. They were 'busy', she'd say if I asked where Dad or Victoria were.

'Go to the park for a bit, Mark.' I'd always go. We all would.

When Victoria was twelve or thirteen she developed a little bit of a belly, and rumours started flying around school. They were saying Vic was pregnant. They were saying it was Dad's baby.

There were too many stories, too much chatter. It was all too open now. Everyone had always known but, until then, they'd known about it in whispers and soft gossip, quiet enough for it to be ignored after a muted chat. Now it was out on the streets.

I wasn't relieved when Dad was taken to prison – I was too young to understand the whole situation. I just knew he was going away and that there'd be even less food in the house. I also knew he was going away because of Victoria, and I'm sorry to say I was angry with her because of that. We all were, but we didn't know any better. Except Mum, she knew better, or she should have anyway, but her concern at the time was keeping Victoria from telling the cops the whole story.

They were the leanest of days, when the old man was in prison, and we got to the point of delirium. I remember all of us in the front room shouting 'HUNGRY' at people while they walked down the street. When they saw us, we'd giggle like hyenas. I guess we were laughing about the contrast between the orderly, peaceful world outside, and the tumult of crap that was going down in our house.

The weird thing is that Mum used to laugh along with us, screaming at the people on the street. That was some crazy shit.

We didn't know what was happening to us was bad. We were kids, and had only ever lived in a household where up was down and wrong was right. All we knew was that Dad was away and there wasn't any food.

Dad came back pretty quickly, after Mum offered Victoria a new bicycle to shut up about the whole thing. I remember we all piled into the car to go and pick him up from the bus stop down at the shops.

We all wanted to see the old man, except Victoria of course. When I first saw him, I felt sorry for him. He had hollow eyes, and a lonely, sad way about him. I'd never seen him like that before.

As soon as he got into the car, though, he slowly started to become himself again, and after a few weeks life pretty much went back to how it had been before, except that Dad lost his job and there was even less food.

Although we were usually in a state of friction, there were some rare moments of fraternity in that house. Steve and John, older and bigger than me, wanted to protect me and especially my sister, even though they didn't really have the capacity. I think that's what fucked them up, and broke something inside their heads.

The old man was God in that house, with a wrath that could equal any ancient, vengeful deity. As little kids there was no defying that. John disappeared into himself and became a quiet, brooding, sometimes morose and often dangerous teenager. Steve started showing signs of being mental. That was what it was called then, 'mental'. Mental wasn't a disease, and there weren't different types of mental, it was just a binary that you'd better fucking try to avoid being on the wrong side of, like being gay, or being dead.

Dad wouldn't suffer a mental son, but when he was twelve it all bubbled over for Steve. He couldn't help but talk nonsense to himself, usually quietly, because if Dad caught him he'd cop a mighty wailing, but sometimes loudly and maniacally. Much later Steve would be diagnosed with schizophrenia. Maybe it was because he had his head slammed into the wall one too many times. I'm no doctor, but I do know about people getting smashed in the head.

At that time, though, the one who was quickly starting to slide away from life was Victoria. Everything that was happening to her had become too much. All that torture, all the shame – she couldn't live with it anymore.

Vic wanted to get away from existence and wherever oblivion could be found – booze, pills, petrol, solvents – she'd go there with no hesitation. She was heading to the darkest of cul-de-sacs until, at fifteen, she found an avenue of escape. And it wasn't one within, but without.

Initially she looked for ways to extend her time away from home. The school day finished at 3 pm, and when she came home Dad would usually be waiting for her, checking her pants, saying that if any of the boys at school ever had their way with her, there'd be hell to pay. After that he'd often exert his dominance, like an animal.

Victoria thought that if she could get to 5 or 6 pm, and if the threat of boys at school was removed, perhaps things might go differently for her. With Dad's consent she quit school and took a job as a machinist at a factory. From there a plan took form.

With money she could escape and get her own place. She wasn't able to keep any of the money she earned at the factory, though, as her wages went straight into Dad's bank account. But maybe she could do some extra hours, and the company would allow her to have that money go into another account?

Her work agreed. The escape was on. Victoria worked, earned, found a room and set a date. Then, just before she was about to leave, the old man found her second bank book. You probably know enough about the old man now to know how he reacted – but Victoria held fast. She was too close to give up.

Eventually Dad offered an olive branch: Victoria would give him all the money in the second account, and he would let her leave. Knowing she'd already paid her bond and advance rent to her new landlord, Vic agreed.

She always knew Dad wouldn't give her up so easily, so she planned to leave without him knowing. When, one day, he came home to find her packed and ready to leave, the shit hit the fan.

Victoria was scared then. I'm not sure he could have done anything worse than what she'd already had to go through and, besides, she was so close to getting away. She'd conceived of life after Dad.

Despite the fact that sibling solidarity was usually in short supply in that fucked-up house, she asked us boys to escort her out of the house, and we agreed. Steve and John made the decision – I was still far too small to defy my dad. Even though they never said it, I'm pretty sure they were proud to finally be able to help.

Victoria left the house with the three of us flanking her as though we were a close protection unit – John and Steve in front, facing Dad, and me, the smallest, behind. John and Steve told Dad that Victoria was leaving and, if he tried to stop her, he was the one who was going to get the beating. It was the first time any of us had defied our father, and the first time we'd ever physically challenged him.

I was still a little kid, but Steve and John were filling out and becoming strong, especially Steve, who was starting his teenage years. The old man could have beaten any one of us then, but not all of us. He had no choice but to let Vic go.

As soon as my sister left the house, Dad jumped in his ute to go after her. Victoria had arranged a lift from the milk boy, Grant, who was sweet on her, and sometimes used to leave flowers with the milk. Grant wasn't due yet, though, so she hid under a tree on a street near ours.

Victoria watched that ute go up and down the surrounding streets until, to her great relief, she saw another familiar vehicle, the one owned by Grant the milk boy.

Vic got away.

I'd love to be able to tell you that Victoria's story was a happy one after that, but it wasn't. Not all of it, anyway. She did survive, though, and survives to this day, and that's something. I know now that growing up like we did, that really does count for something.

Chapter 2

SOUTH AUCKLAND, NEW ZEALAND
1990

Everyone round the neighbourhood knew that family, and those
Hunt boys. They were known as being tough bastards [who]
could all handle themselves. Steve was known as the toughest
of them all; John was a bit of an angry dude; and Mark, well
Mark was like . . . the kid. Big kid, rough kid, but a kid.

JONATHON AFIAKI (FRIEND)

When I was little, I couldn't really recognise how I felt. My kids these days can tell you if they're sad, or happy, or hopeful, or disappointed, or whatever – in fact, some days they won't shut up about it – but it wasn't like that then. It wasn't like that for me, anyway.

When I was a kid, I could tell you when I was hungry, or in physical pain, but besides that I probably wouldn't have been able to tell you much about how I felt. We didn't talk like that in my house, and we didn't think like that. I didn't really have an emotional vocabulary until later in life.

If I could articulate myself properly when I went to school, I probably would have told you that I was always embarrassed. As soon as I had classmates with normal lives, I was embarrassed by that house, by the old man, by the fact that we didn't have any food and, most of all, those rumours that were going around.

I used to cry on the way to primary school. I'd be dressed in Steve's or John's hand-me-down clothes, and sometimes even Victoria's, knowing that I had all those miserable hours ahead of me, often obsessing about the worst part of the school day: lunchtime.

When the rest of the kids were going to be tucking into sandwiches, Fruit Boxes and Milky Ways, I was going to be sitting there on my own, hungry and bitter. Sometimes Dad would save me by coming in and dropping off some lunch for me, but it very rarely happened. That'd be one of the few times I'd look forward to seeing him.

Sometimes the teachers and other kids would pity me and throw me a sandwich half or some fruit. I appreciated the food, but never the pity. I was never, ever in for the pity. I guess I must have felt pride then, too. You can't have embarrassment without pride.

I had a funny relationship with most of my primary school mates. We weren't really peers, so we couldn't ever really be mates. If you saw my school photos, I was a scowl in a sea of smiles. I didn't have much to smile about.

It was at primary school that I first developed a temper that could burn a hole in the floor. Add that temper to the fact that there was only one authority figure at the time that meant anything – a teacher's stern words and detentions meant jack shit compared to the old man's fists – and I wasn't destined to have much of an academic career.

For me, school wasn't a place of learning and enrichment, it was just a place I had to be at from Monday to Friday. The teachers had to be endured, as did other kids, but it did have benefits, like if someone was going to get fucked up at school, it sure as hell wasn't going to be me.

I remember the first time I had a go at someone at school. It was this kid, Alex, who, in the third or fourth grade class, said something that got my back up. I don't remember exactly what he said to me, but I remember desperately wanting to say something sharp and cutting back to him. My mind was fuzzy, though. Nothing came but frustration. My annoyance grew and grew until I picked this poor little dude up with both hands and hurled him across the classroom.

He landed like a bag of garbage, and there was a sound in the room.

Ooooooohhhhhhh.

I remember how light that kid felt, how small. I remember the dawning realisation that I was stronger than this kid, and possibly stronger than all of them. I hadn't been strong in my house but, at school, there were possibilities of physical domination.

Throwing that little smart-ass across the room felt good. I didn't feel any remorse, and I didn't give a shit about what was going to happen to me when the teachers turned up on the scene.

I just remember feeling the power of it. This was probably the first time in my life that I'd felt empowered. It might have also been the first time that the embarrassment of my existence started to recede.

I realised at primary school that I had no verbal defence for anything anyone said to me. I *was* wearing girl's clothes, and I *was* as hungry as a stray dog. I *was* a poor-ass coconut (New Zealand's favourite racist taunt for Polynesians), living in a house of abuse and beatings. That was all true. But I could also pick you up and throw you across the room if I really wanted to. That was a pretty good equaliser as far as I was concerned.

It wasn't like I was accepted after I started asserting myself physically at school, or even respected, but when I wanted people to avoid me, then they would. That would do for me.

I didn't really hate primary school. Some of the teachers were kind to me – usually middle-aged Pakeha women with sensible shoes and mid-length hair – and I preferred the sense and structure of those school days to the chaos of home.

I really hated high school, though. I guess, overall, primary school is a journey towards high school, a journey all us kids were taking together. High school, though, that was a journey into the early days of adult life. Some of us wouldn't be completing that journey yet. Some of us would end up in a void between school and life that would cast us as outsiders.

There were a couple of things I liked to do at high school, it just turned out that none of those things happened in a classroom. I liked to sleep in the big tree out on the oval (the one where I could see if Dad was coming for me); I liked jimmying 50-cent pieces out of the tennis court vending machine; and I also liked to play rugby league.

League was a natural fit for me. I was big for my age, strong, quick on my feet and unfazed by the licks that you had to take playing the game. The boys used to play rugby at lunchtime. Sometimes I'd join the game, sometimes I'd ruin the game. When I wanted to ruin the game, I'd take the ball and slowly walk back to my try line. Then, even more slowly, I'd walk towards the opposition try line, daring someone to try to tackle me. If anyone ever did, they'd get their ass beaten.

It was the world's stupidest way of playing rugby, especially for someone like me who really enjoyed competition and was genuinely good at the game. I can justify a lot of what I did as a kid, but I can't for the life of me remember why I played rugby like that. It was a dumb way of playing the game, and an even worse way of making friends but, oddly, I did.

When I met Johnno, he was new to our school, having been kicked out of his class for belting a teacher. Maybe he didn't understand the way I played rugby, maybe he did; either way, when he and his friend Derek saw me walking slowly with the ball, they ran straight at me. After they bounced off me, I whipped both their asses. Johnno didn't care. First he fought back and when he couldn't anymore, he just stood there and took it. In him I saw familiarity; this wasn't the first beating this kid had ever suffered. Right there and then on the oval, we became friends.

It was with Johnno that I first made myself known to the cops. I'd been coveting all the things the other kids took for granted my whole life: food, shoes, bikes, T-shirts, video games. Now, with Johnno, I realised all I needed to do to get these things was just go out there and grab them.

The first time the cops picked me up was for stealing shoes. I was at one of the malls near my house when Johnno noticed that one of the shoe shops had an open window that led to the car park. While I was handing a pair of shoes – Timberlands, I think – out to Johnno, a couple of big, meaty man-hands clamped down on me. The store security guard held me at the shop until the police turned up. The cops threatened me with this or that, but I didn't give a shit about whatever they were going to be levelling at me; I was only worried about how badly I was going to get beaten when my old man found out.

That scene was repeated over and over again, and soon I even stopped worrying about how badly I was going to get beaten when Dad had to turn up at the cop shop. Those beatings were notes in a symphony. In trouble with the police or not, I was always in line to get the shit beaten out of me, regardless of what was going on.

In my latter high school years, school started to become physically unbearable. If I went to all the classes I was supposed to go to, then I'd spend all of my time being bored and angry at school, or terrorised and despairing at home.

Fuck that. I was going to carve some time out for me. By the time I went to secondary school, you would've been more likely to find me at the school grounds on the weekend than you would've during the week. It was at school on a Saturday where I met Simi and Eti, a couple of tough Samoan kids who were a bit older than me, and a little bit further down the path of delinquency. After I met those guys things began to get a little bit out of control. I hadn't been hanging out with them for long when I started turning up in the dock of the children's court.

'I'm sorry. I won't do it again. I've learned.' Blah blah blah.

It was also then that I started to fight. Stealing was a pretty decent way to gain respect in my South Auckland circles, but the best way to get respect was being able to scrap.

I lost my first fistfight. I can't remember what it was about, which isn't surprising because most fights in those days weren't about much more than a willingness to throw down. I do remember walking away wondering why people made such a big deal out of it, though. There was a little bit of activity; fists flew, I got hit a lot, he didn't. It probably wasn't even the worst ass-kicking I'd had that week. When it was all over, I knew I had absolutely nothing to fear from fistfighting.

The circumstances of my second street fight would repeat themselves quite a lot in my life. I was late to the scene of that scrap. Eti was already in a brawl, and was being outgunned by a guy who was a little bit older and a lot larger than him. I ploughed into that fight with open eyes and ready fists. That was a short scrap, that one.

I was barely a teenager then, and less than half the size I am now, but after I'd swung my fist, that guy across from me fell – one punch and he was out cold. Damn, that was a good feeling. There had been a problem, and I was the solution. Good feeling that, great feeling.

Before that I'd been Simi and Eti's bum boy, going and buying stuff for them, laughing at their jokes, scrounging cigarettes for them and generally being a lower-class friend. After showing my talent with my fists, I became an asset. Every group of young fellas in South Auckland needed someone like me, someone who could do the scrapping, and if it could be a kid, even better. If our kid can fuck you up, then what chance do you have against the rest of us?

It was also with Simi and Eti that I started boosting cars. The first car I stole was a Datsun 180B, and I kept stealing those Dattos for years. The Datto was attractive to the car-buying public in South Auckland for the same reason it was attractive to us kids – it was durable and cheap to run (yeah, we did quite often have to put petrol in our stolen rides). That car also had the added bonus of being easy to jack. Just an elbow into the quarter window, a fork in the ignition and you were away, into the night.

I remember being in that first Datsun, with the boys and one of their uncles – a guy maybe the age I am now – and thinking that I was the coolest motherfucker in all of the North Island. This was some adult shit, and I was smack-bang in the middle of it. I was part of something.

We weren't involved in commercial car theft – we weren't selling these cars, stripping them, rebirthing them, nothing like that – this was just about utility, and shits and giggles. I loved it, though. I loved the freedom, the escape and the camaraderie of it all. With a stolen car you could go anywhere you wanted, and with that little bit of illicit electricity running through your veins throughout the trip.

I must have stolen dozens and dozens of cars in my early teens. There was no reason not to. I never thought about the legal shit I could get dumped in and I certainly didn't give a fuck about the sanctity of someone else's stuff. I'd never known the pleasure of having any property worth owning then, so I didn't know what it meant to lose something you cherished.

The cars usually did come back to South Auckland – we did need to get home after all. Sometimes those cars would end up on the side of the road, sometimes in a park, but usually I dumped the cars on the oval of my old school, after having tested how far my ride could fly past the little hump near the rugby pitch.

There were occasions, though, that the cars didn't come back. One night Johnno and I boosted a couple of cars. Each in our own vehicles, we decided to cruise down to the Otahuhu rugby clubrooms. That night, though, it seemed the stolen-car juice in our veins was running just a little too hot.

I stopped at the traffic lights in the old Corolla shitbox I'd jacked, waiting for Johnno's Datsun to catch up to me. When I saw the headlights of his vehicle in my rearview mirror, they were coming at an alarming pace. Soon I felt a violent jolt and heard the crunch of metal on metal.

This fuckin' guy.

When I gathered myself, I looked behind and saw a maniacal grinning face in the car behind me.

Going to be like that is it, bro?

We were racing now. I took off down the street and when Johnno pulled his Datsun alongside, both engines over-revving, I yanked the steering wheel towards him and smashed my ride into his. When he caught up he smashed back, and there we were, barging the shit out of those cars, crashing into each other all the way to Otahuhu, as though it was the end point of some hyper-realistic driving game.

As the cars were hitting each other, I could see sparks in the darkness and heard the scream of side panels colliding. For anyone walking the quiet, dark streets of South Auckland that night, it would have been quite the spectacle seeing us fly past.

When I saw the slip road to the clubrooms I slowed down, but before I could turn in, Johnno's Datsun careened into the back of me, smashing me through a fence and into the front yard of a house.

Shortly another link was added to the chain of smashed-up vehicles, when a civilian, surprised by Johnno's abrupt stop, banged into the back of his Datsun. I ditched my car and ran off to the rugby pitch. From the darkness, I watched the foot race between Johnno and the guys who had smashed into the back of his car.

'Good luck fella,' I laughed quietly.

He did have good luck, managing to boost another car that was parked at the clubrooms – a VW Beetle – and race off into the night. Later on the fella who owned the VW figured out that it was my crew who had taken his car. Johnno sent out the word that it was me who'd boosted it. If the guy caught up with me, it'd be on, and Johnno knew that. Better me in a scrap than Johnno, I guess.

I didn't mind. It was always better to have me in a scrap than any of the other boys. Things were like that in

South Auckland then, a patchwork of beefs and resentments which, when the alignment was right, resulted in bursts of violence. It was hard to keep up with it all sometimes. There was more than one occasion when I'd see a bloke and have to go through the old mental Rolodex to see how likely it'd be that he'd be coming over with something swinging towards my head – fists usually, but sometimes a bat or a chain. Grudges could stretch out through generations where I came from, but they could also be happily quashed once the fists flew.

In those early teenage years I first rubbed up against a group of fellas who would keep crossing my path for years. It was supposed to be a pre-arranged fight: because of some long-forgotten slight, Simi would be scrapping against a kid from another school named Siaosi. The agreed terms were that this was going to be a one-on-one affair, with Eti and me there for moral support. When we got to the scrap, though, we found a mob that looked like one of the gangs from the movie *The Warriors* – literally dozens of fellas, with all kinds of blunt instruments.

Those guys were sick of our shit. We'd put hands on too many of the guys from their school and they weren't there for a fight, they were there for a lynching. Seeing their numbers and anger, we ran. I would get to put fists on a couple of them many years later, but by then I no longer fought with malice.

That lynch mob had included Samoan brothers Clay and Auckland Auimatagi, who lived nearby and trained at a kickboxing gym run by trainer Lolo Heimuli. The gym boasted a group of Islander kids who would become world-class fighters, with the best of them being another pair of Samoan brothers, Ray and Rony Sefo. Clay, Auckland and Rony would become opponents, rivals and friends; Lolo is one of my current trainers and Ray, well, Ray would make me famous.

At that time, though, I still only fought for fun. While they were training, I was stealing, robbing, mugging and generally running wild. I wasn't scared of the police and the courts – when they grabbed me, I'd be back out on the streets in no time – and I wasn't scared of the other guys in the neighbourhood. As far as I was concerned, I'd become untouchable.

I never for a moment thought about injury or death, but in retrospect I guess either of those could have been a possibility. On one occasion when I jacked a car with a few mates in South Auckland, we headed into town, where the mugging spoils were always better. We pulled up in a side street in Newmarket, a busy entertainment and shopping district in central Auckland, and split up into two pairs, with each team heading off to see what we could bring back. I returned with some skinned knuckles and a wallet, waiting for the other fellas to come back. The minutes dragged, until I heard a noise getting louder and louder.

waaaahhhhaAAHGGGRAAAHHHH

It wasn't a cop's siren, or a screaming victim, but something else. A mate of mine named Brigham had done the stand-and-deliver on a bloke, who, in turn, had reached into his bag and pulled out a chainsaw. Those boys ran like bloody Leatherface himself was chasing them. While we piled into the car and peeled away, the chainsaw fella was still coming at us. I'm not sure that we stopped laughing all the way back to Papatoetoe.

That stuff was all a laugh to me and nothing more. From the outside it might have looked like I was battling with society, but I wasn't Chuck D or Tupac Shakur. It wasn't me against the world, and I wasn't fighting the power, I was just amusing myself. My real fight was always at home.

You're probably imagining that my brothers were up to the same kind of nefarious shit that I was getting into then, but that wasn't the case. Rough and tough as they were, my brothers were both hardworking and conscientious. While I was escaping the house by being a fuck-up and a criminal, John was escaping it by studying and reading, and Steve was playing sports, where he excelled. You probably think that their way was healthier than mine, but if you look at the outcomes, perhaps that's not the case.

Steve was the first one to break. I guess he must have been the most brittle of us kids, and one day his brain just snapped. It happened after his girl, Donna, broke up with him. Young as I was, I knew it wasn't her that actually did him in. That break-up was just a straw on the back of a camel that had been laden with a whole childhood of shit.

The first I knew about it was when I got a call from Donna. We didn't always have a home phone, but we did then, and she called and said that Steve had just walked into her house, silently and with no expression, before sitting down on the couch in front of the television. Donna said that there was no talking to him, and no moving him. He was just sitting there, like a statue, staring at *Fair Go*, or the news or whatever. That would have been quite the dilemma for anyone: Steve was the biggest and strongest of all of us.

I was still much too young to drive then (although we've established that I knew how), but I got in my dad's car that night and drove over straight away. When I got there, I found a terrified family, and no recognition or focus in Steve's eyes. Donna said they'd done everything they could to get my brother out of their lounge room, but once I said, 'Let's go' to him, he simply got up and left with me.

He had nothing to say to me on the way home. He had nothing much to say to any of us after that, reserving most conversation for the people who lived in his head.

When the old man realised he couldn't beat the mental out of Steve, he shipped him off to Kingseat Hospital, a grim, pre-war loony bin, which has now been closed as a hospital, but reopened as supposedly the most haunted place in New Zealand. Shortly after he came out of Kingseat, Steve was on the streets: a schizophrenic homeless sixteen-year-old having his own battles every day. I remember seeing him a few months later on the street – shirt off, screaming obscenities, punching himself in the head. I really wished I could have done more for Steve. I couldn't, though. I was just a kid, and every day I just thought about me. I had to.

When Steve got shipped off, there were only two of us left in the house. A few years after that, there would be none.

Like I said, although I had stopped going to school on weekdays, I still liked getting down there on the weekend, hanging out with the boys and seeing whatever shit we could get into. In one instance, that shit arrived in the form of a pair of nice, shiny Doc Martens shoes, worn by a kid a little older than me, who was hanging out with some of his buddies.

This kid was asking for a robbing, but I saw it as at least a three-man job, and I was down at the school with just my mate Troy. I quickly ran around the friendly houses to see if I could enlist any of my usual co-conspirators, but no one was home. As I ran back to the school, I stopped by my house, where I found John.

John usually looked down on the criminal shit I was into, and I can't remember what I said to get him to go with me. I probably just told him I needed help. Even though he could get explosively angry with me, John usually tried to help me with whatever if he could.

I was happy to find the kid with the Doc Martens still at the school and, after beating on him a little, I was soon wearing nice, new, snug-fitting Docs. It was a situation I'd been in countless times, but the difference this time was that the shoeless dude went straight to the cops. It wasn't hard for them to identify John and me, as it turned out the guys we mugged had been in the same year at school as John. John didn't remember those kids, but they remembered him.

My eyes would generally glaze over when I was dragged to court, only coming alive when it was time for me to offer up my lines of contrition, and a promise to mend my childhood ways. This time, though, there was no space for me to speak, just a barking from the bench.

'Nine and a half months,' the magistrate said.

'Nine and a half months of what?' I asked.

'You're going to prison, son.'

I had a pretty long rap sheet by then, but it was still surprising. I'm not saying I didn't deserve it – I was a fucking menace, no doubt – but if I'd been busted for car theft, or assault, or kidnapping or almost any other crime, they probably wouldn't have sent me, a sixteen-year-old kid, into a real, adult jail. Stealing shoes, though, that was the end of civilisation as we knew it. That particular crime was selling papers back then, and formed the crest of a moral panic washing over the whole Western world. Something had to be done about it. Something *was* done about it. John copped a custodial sentence, too, but a shorter one because he didn't have the criminal history that his younger brother did. When they took me from the dock I wasn't scared, nor was I excited. I wasn't thinking much, just that I was about to find out what jail was like. I don't know how John felt about being shipped off to prison, because I never talked to him about it. I can imagine he was pretty pissed off, though. While prison was possibly going to be a useful experience in my future as a fuck-up, it wasn't going to be a useful experience for John who, at that point, had a chance of further education and possibly even a regular life.

I don't spend a lot of time thinking about shit I did as a teenager, regretting the decisions I made or feeling bad about the people I hurt. I do think about my decision to pester John that afternoon, though, and I do wonder how things might have turned out for him if I hadn't.

We were sent to different prisons: John to Mount Eden Prison, a nineteenth-century monolith of a jail, and me to Waikeria Corrections Facility, then New Zealand's largest prison. Waikeria was probably the place where my childhood ended. My immaturity would continue for decades, but once you go to an adult prison, it's hard to stay a kid.

Although the time I spent in Waikeria was probably the least violent in my life at that point, I did get belted the day I got in there. It was a screw who hit me, while I was drawing on my arm in a lame attempt to look like the rest of the real men with real tattoos

'You cut that shit out, kid,' he barked with a finger in my face. I did.

It occurred to me then that this dude had the ultimate level of control over me. I was getting pretty big, so not even Dad had that level of control over me anymore. This guy, though, he could do whatever he wanted to do to me in this place.

A few hours after that, another level of prison control revealed itself when I got into gen-pop. I was talking to this Pakeha dude – shaved head, gothic tatts and also fresh to Waikeria – and out of the blue, one of the prisoners walking past just launched at him. The stranger took him off the bench, onto the ground and just started whaling into him with punches.

It wasn't like that outside. Outside there'd usually be words or stares before the fists came. Here it was just a storm from blue skies.

'Why were you talking to that guy?' the puncher asked me after he'd finished with his prey. I said I didn't know. He was just a guy.

'Well fucking don't, kid. Stick with your own.'

There were new rules, and one of those was that a coconut like me wasn't going to be talking to any skinheads. The guy who was doing the punching was named Jinx, and he was one of the alpha males in the joint. I was going to be following his lead. That was going to work for me.

Like most prisons around the world, the gangs ran Waikeria, and if they decided to mess with you, then prison wasn't going to be much fun. Thankfully, the gangs didn't mess with me, and I quickly learned all the rules of the place. Things were especially easy for me perhaps because I was at the bottom of the heap – I was a kid after all. There really wasn't much point in fucking me up.

I ended up having a pretty good time in prison. It felt like a holiday. There were three square meals a day – that was my favourite part – and work at the nearby dairy farm, and weights, and 'crash', which was a jail version of rugby league played on cement and sometimes – in my case, anyway – barefoot.

I was one of the better crash players in prison, and that gave me some social currency among the inmates. More came when Josh Mataulfati, a gang leader and one of the prison's toughest guys, took me on as a sort of personal assistant and training lackey. Mataulfati was a kickboxer, and gave me the job of organising his gear and holding the bag for him while he trained.

I'd always loved my kung fu films, but this was the first time I'd seen martial arts for real. Josh was a good kickboxer: his strikes were precise, deliberate and well thought out. I appreciated the artistry and power of his punches, and I loved the *boom* when a good kick landed on the bag.

You might be thinking it was here that I saw a future in those martial arts for myself. You might also be thinking that I saw a future in crime, but in both cases you'd be mistaken. I never threw one punch in prison, not in anger, nor on a bag or pad. I wasn't thinking about any future in prison at all, I was just enjoying a break from the chaos my life had been.

One day after he finished training, Josh asked me if I wanted to 'nom up' (start the nomination process) for his gang the Mongrel Mob. Up to that point I'd never thought about what I wanted out of life, but this offer forced me to think ahead. Nomming up was committing to a certain life, and a certain code.

'Nah, I'm right.' That's what I told Josh.

Even though I'd be coming out of jail a sixteen-year-old, uneducated, penniless, convicted criminal, I felt like I could get more out of this life than crime, gangs and prisons. I eventually ended up being right, but man, for a while there it was a close-run thing.

Chapter 3

SOUTH AUCKLAND, NEW ZEALAND
1992

There were only a few great upcoming league players knocking
around Auckland at the time; one of them was Ruben Wiki,
and another was Mark. Mark played in the front row, ran
like a winger and hit like a freight train. He could have been
one of the greats in the NRL, I got no doubt about that. As
awesome as he could have been at league, that guy was
born to fight. They say that fighters are made, not born,
and that's true for everyone I've ever seen, except Mark.

DAVE FUIMOANA (FRIEND)

It had only been a few months, but when I got out of
Waikeria I felt like I had crossed some kind of threshold.
I felt older. I felt tougher. I felt less like a boy and more
like a man, for better or for worse.

45

In prison, I met the real *hombres*. Not the bored shoe stealers and the drunken joyriders I'd hung out with up to then, but the real-deal criminals – the dudes who did the heists and the shakedowns, the guys who sold the drugs and stuffed people in car boots.

When I got out of prison, no one was going to tell me what to do. Before prison, the group of fellas I'd rolled with had me as their heavy-fisted lackey, but now I refused to be anyone's bitch.

Prison had put me over a hump with my dad, too. After my release I lived at home for a while, but he didn't have the power he'd had before. He, like most other blokes then, didn't have the stomach for stepping to me anymore.

My mum was almost a stranger to me then, too, but I do remember one day when she stopped me with concern in her eyes and said, 'Son, I heard about that bank that got robbed this week. Was it your gang that did it?'

I laughed right in her face. She really didn't know shit about me. Robbing banks was not ripping off shit-box cars and belting other teenagers. I went to leave, still laughing, but she grabbed me on my way out.

'If it was, you have to give me some of that money, right?'

That's when the laughter really took off – peals and peals of it. I do feel sorry for my mum, and on my most generous days even my dad. They never learned to be good adults, no one ever taught them. They lived a hardscrabble life, and it sent them wild in their own way. It's not an excuse, but at least it made sense.

I enjoyed my new post-prison status, but I also came out craving some of the structure I'd experienced inside. In prison, I'd been put to work at a nearby dairy farm, and even though it was tough, stinky work, I got a lot out of it. I needed dates on the calendar to remember, something to strive towards. I took a couple of regular jobs in that period. I worked at a Mobil petrol station, and I also started to take my rugby a little more seriously, joining my first club side, the Mangere East Hawks.

As I described earlier, when I played rugby at school I played like a dickhead, disrespecting the rules of the game and the other players. Now I understood that only within the parameters of the game could I really test myself. That's what I wanted to do. I was good, and now I wanted to know how good.

I played in the forwards, and while there were a lot of big, strong Polynesian blokes in that competition – including future heavyweight boxing legend David Tua, who also went to my school – I found myself pretty mobile compared to a lot of them.

After prison, I also started to generate a little bit of rep interest. I was picked for the Auckland under-nineteen rugby league team, and there was some talk of me getting a start in the Junior Kiwis, who were touring England later in the year. That would have been an honour, and I hadn't had any of those in my life at that point. Even now, with more years living in Australia than New Zealand, an Australian family and Samoan blood in my veins, I still consider myself a New Zealander. No matter what happens in life I will always be a Kiwi, and being picked to represent that country in rugby league would have been a big deal to me.

They didn't want me, though. I started hearing that the coaches had found out I was a crim, and not just a junior criminal (there were plenty of those in league), but a felon with prison time under my belt. After that, the talk of me being picked for a rep side cooled.

One day the coaches sat me down and said it'd probably be too difficult for me to get a visa to tour overseas, and perhaps I should shelve the idea of rep rugby. I'd worked hard at my league but after that conversation, I walked home from training with my mate Dave and decided I was done with it.

'If they don't want me, then fuck them and fuck their sport,' I told him.

I was done with the petrol station job, too. Fuck the long nights, fuck my neon tan, fuck 'three dollars fifty on pump nine'. Fuck it all.

I went back to robbing then, and I also thought about getting into drug dealing. There was a weed dealer round our parts named Barton who was a mate of mine and he seemed to do a brisk trade in tinnies, so I took Dave along with me to see if we could help him with his business.

Barton acted like Scarface on the streets, but when I went round to his place, I tell you, it was no Miami mansion. His place was tiny, and looked smaller because there were piles of crap everywhere – clothes, dishes, pizza boxes. There was also shit on the roof – yes, actual shit. How it got there, I have no idea.

Barton was happy for me to help him out, but having visited his joint, I wasn't so sure anymore. The idea completely died a week later when Barton got batted up by some of his competitors. Next time I saw him, he had all kinds of surgery scars. Maybe that's why he was so keen to get me into his enterprise.

I took another menial job working at a factory and soon my weeks and months were held up by the tent poles of weekend drinking sessions with the lads, robberies of various stripes and a shitload more street fighting. If you weren't there in South Auckland in the nineties, you probably don't understand how it worked. Wherever you were, a fight was only one glance away, one look at any moment. That's how it usually started, with a look. Sometimes you threw that look because of a real slight – perhaps someone had said something to your girl, or one of her friends, or maybe there was money owed, or you'd smashed a friend of theirs, or they'd smashed your friend. Sometimes the look was just because you were bored or because you'd had a shitty day, and someone had to pay for it.

Either way, when someone threw that look over to you, you had two options – you could pretend you didn't see and bitch out, or you could throw over a look of your own. When you did that, it was on.

As my body grew bigger I started fighting every week, and I just got better and better at it. I can't account for all of why I'm good at fighting, but some of it is that I don't really feel pain, not like most people do. I know I can never feel what other people feel, and other people can't feel what I feel, but I really don't think we can feel it the same way, because otherwise others wouldn't be so scared of it.

I vaguely remember what it felt like when Dad started beating the shit out of me. It's not something I'm familiar with now, even when I'm being pounded by dudes like Junior dos Santos or Stipe Miocic. At some point as a little kid, I managed to take pain and put it somewhere outside my head. It existed somewhere, but not anywhere it could stop my fight.

I didn't really ever get injured then, either. I'd hear people I scrapped with copped broken jaws, busted noses, fractured eye sockets, broken ribs, but me, I was always golden. If I didn't feel pain and didn't get hurt, why wouldn't I scrap? I fought in the city, in the south, in the suburbs. I fought at schools, I fought in bars, I fought in the street, but it was one day, fighting out the front of a club, where someone noticed and my life started to take a nice little turn. It took me nearly another decade after that brawl to realise how significant it was, but isn't that how real life works? It's only ever looking backwards that you can see whether a road you've taken was a road to fortune or ruin.

That night started pretty much like all the rest. Johnno and I were up to our regular brand of mischief – we found a few fellas on Karangahape Road, just north of the city, with a jacket and watch we liked the look of. We gave those fellas a whipping, stole their gear and then headed to Don't Tell Mama's nightclub nearby for some celebratory drinks.

All was good at DTMs – a little Bobby Brown on the decks and the drinks were flowing – until I realised I hadn't seen Johnno for a little while. After a bit of asking around, I was told Johnno had gone out the front of the club with some angry-looking fellas. In fact, the dude had been frog-marched.

Outside the club I found a scrum of guys putting the boot into Johnno, who was on the ground in a ball. I ran over to help, but slipped and soon I was on the ground next to him, copping my own kicking.

The police turned up on the scene, dragging these fellas off us. They put themselves between us and these fellas, some of whom we'd robbed earlier. The cops started asking questions, but of course no one was answering. I'm guessing we were close to being given a stern talking-to and told to piss off, but that old anger started to burn hotter than reason or consequence could possibly cool.

I could still feel their kicks on me and see the foot scuffs on my clothes. What were they, these fellas, to me? What gave them the right to put their boots into me? WHO THE FUCK ARE YOU?

While one of the cops was jibber-jabbering, I moved slowly towards one of the guys who'd been kicking me and I let fly with a big right hand. The fella was out before he even landed, falling under the wheels of the police car. Then I reloaded and dropped one of his mates, and then one more after that.

Soon it was mayhem out on the street. Johnno and I were into it, and the fellas on the other side, but also people who'd come from nowhere. It became one of those scraps no one wanted to miss. The cops were trying to get a handle on the whole ruckus, but they realised they needed back-up, and they were calling for it on their radios.

While the street was all flying fists and shouting, a hand reached over and pulled me back into the club. It was a dreadlocked guy, shorter and older than me, but strong, tattooed and with a definite confidence. This guy pushed me into the staff toilets and told me to stay there until he came and got me. I did what he said, and waited there for what felt like an hour. When the door opened, I knew this guy had probably just kept me from another stint in prison.

'So, you like a scrap, do you son?' the man asked.

I didn't say anything.

'You want a real fight then?'

I did wonder what I'd been doing up to that point. The man said the words *Muay Thai*, but it didn't mean anything to me. He said the word 'kickboxing', which I did understand. Then he said the word 'Thursday'.

'This Thursday?' I asked.

'This Thursday, bro.'

'Where?'

'Here. You in?'

This guy's name was Sam Marsters, a bouncer at DTMs and a few other clubs around K'Road. He was also a fighter, a trainer and a bit of a local entrepreneur. In five days' time, Marsters wanted me to have a kickboxing fight in this nightclub. I was in.

There have been a few people over the years who've reached into the sloppy mess of my life, pulled me out and put me on some solid ground, and Sam Marsters was probably the first. He invited me to go to his gym in Fort Street for a little bit of training, and the two things I remember about that place are the smell of liniment, and learning how to throw a punch into a pad, which was pretty much all I did learn. After all, five days is five days.

Sam Marsters is a cool cat. Even though he was only ten or so years older than me, he had lived a life, having worked as a free-diving fisherman at his ancestral home, the Cook Islands; run a plantation in PNG; and fought some of the world's best fighters in the discipline of *Muay Thai*, which is a variation on kickboxing that allows elbow and knee strikes.

I liked Sam from the get-go. He was honest, quiet, strong, fair and left no doubt as to who was in charge in his presence.

When I walked into DTMs the next Thursday, the place had been transformed. The dance floor had been cleared of baggy-pant- and short-skirt-wearing teenagers to make way for a boxing ring. The crowd had been converted too, from party kids to an older, uglier crowd, and when I came out from the toilets and towards the ring, I saw mullets, prison tatts and gappy smiles either side of me.

Sam had taught me what he could, but I had pretty much no training, and no one expects an eighteen-year-old kid with no training to win an organised fight. I walked to the ring almost completely free of stress, feeling calm even when I got there and found a much larger Islander, older and certainly more experienced than me. Surely if this guy started beating the daylights out of me, someone would stop it.

'Oh shit,' I kept thinking to myself over and over again. Not, 'Oh shit, how did I get into this?' Or, 'Oh shit, how do I get out of this?' Just, 'Oh shit I'm here in a *Muay Thai* fight in a nightclub and everyone is staring at me.'

It was a very strange feeling and, I tell you, I didn't mind the attention at all. When the announcer said my name, people started cheering, not because anyone knew who I was, but because I was one of Sam's guys, fighting in one of Sam's events. I was the hometown boy and I liked their cheers.

When the bell rang, it felt strange to be wearing gloves, but other than that I felt comfortable. For a good part of the first round I only threw punches, but later I thought I should throw in a few kicks, because, you know, this was a kickboxing fight after all.

After my untrained shin slapped into my opponent's leg and a shock ran up through my body, I realised that these kicks were probably slowing me more than him so I went back to punches.

As time ticked past through the first round, I grew more and more confident. Fighting just one guy, on a flat surface, with no bins or kerbs to fall over was actually pretty easy going.

When I came out for the second round I was ready to look for that spot where his chin would be open for business. With naked fists and often wildly swinging opponents, it was much easier to find that spot on the streets, but I was confident, with a little patience, that I'd get to this guy's spot. A scenario started playing in my mind. The ring was the same, but beyond it wasn't a nightclub, it was a stadium – the MGM Grand Garden Arena. There were thousands of people and lights and cameras, and I was stacked with muscles. I was darker skinned, too. I was Mike Tyson. My head had been playing a news clip I'd seen on TV of Mike Tyson knocking some poor fella out. It was a clean, one-punch knockout, but which punch was it?

Then I saw it – a naked jaw and dropped hands. I threw a straight right at my opponent, landing it square on the jaw. It was the same punch as the one I'd seen Iron Mike throw, and the results were the same. This dude was out cold. The crowd cheered and shouted, saying only good things, nice things.

'They need to put this kid in the movies,' a woman yelled. A ripple of laughter followed. It felt good. It felt really good. I started dancing around the ring – we were in a nightclub, after all.

'Good shit, son,' Sam said to me after the fight, handing me a six-pack. Those beers didn't last long.

'You know, I reckon we should probably do this again.'

I reckoned he was right.

Chapter 4

AUCKLAND, NEW ZEALAND
1994

I told my wife at the time, 'I'm going to get a crew of hoods and
street kids together and I don't care how bad they are, I'm going to
bring 'em in and turn 'em into fighters. Try to make 'em better people.'
I was brought up on the streets and no one taught me shit, and I was
going to teach these kids some of the stuff I wish I'd been taught.

SAM MARSTERS (TRAINER)

After that first fight Marsters left me an open invitation to
train with him for free at his little gym on Fort Street in
the Auckland CBD. I was an infrequent visitor, but it was
at that spartan place where I first learned to bring a little
control to my fighting, a little discipline. My fighting style
didn't change – it's never really changed, not even now – but
that was where I started to learn ring craft.

I enjoyed training at Sam's gym, but it never felt part of my real life. My real life was still all that mayhem in the south. The gym was a nice, safe harbour, but it wasn't in my country and I'd only visit it when the current took me there.

One day Sam bailed me up at the gym and asked me why I didn't train more often. He knew I was enjoying it and that I liked the rest of the guys, and I was getting pretty good at it, too. He just didn't understand.

When I told him about my life outside the gym, just a little, Sam suggested I move into the warehouse he was fitting out as his new gym. He said Dave could move in too.

Why not, eh?

The warehouse started as a big empty space with a ring in the middle, but grew into a home of sorts, with a few partitions bearing some posters of fighters or girls, and a few Pakeha housemates, many of whom had come off the streets, and even some food in the fridge from time to time.

Life there was good, and I liked the other guys I lived and trained with. Discipline wasn't particularly strict – Sam knew most of the boys he'd taken on had some issues with authority – but what rules did exist were enforced enthusiastically, and the big one was that when you were at the gym, you had to respect the gym, respect your gym mates and, above all, respect Sam.

We had free rein to do whatever we wanted outside the gym – and there were some crazy lives being lived outside that gym (one of those Pakeha dudes was even getting paid to root older women) – but inside the gym we had to be cool.

We were all shits in our own way, though, and sometimes we ran foul of Sam. When that happened, we'd probably end up in the ring with him. Shortly after you'd be waking up. Sam never knocked me out, though. Not because I was never asking for it, but because it wasn't an easy thing to do. With me, he'd use his grappling skills to establish who was the boss. I hated that. Not the discipline, mind you – Sam was nothing like the old man, and I always understood why he did what he did – but I hated the powerlessness of being stuck in a strong, talented grappler's embrace.

When I was living at Sam's gym I started travelling around the country a little. In addition to the fight shows he promoted at his clubs, Sam used to offset the cost of running his gym by plugging us into events his mates were organising.

'What do you need? A 62, an 82 and a heavyweight? Can do – they're right here at my gym,' I'd hear him bark into his mobile, and off we'd go to some event somewhere.

Sam would also take us on road trips to places like Piha and Muriwai Beaches on the West Coast, where the surf was good, breaking on gorgeous black sand beaches. He was a mad keen surfer, Sam Marsters – still is actually – and so were a lot of the other fighters.

I got on a board a few times, but I wasn't a great swimmer and was probably a bit too big for those boards, so the surfing bug never bit me. I still loved those trips, though, when all of us piled into a car stacked with food, weed and booze for a few days of fun. It was like being part of the Teenage Mutant Ninja Turtles.

I was particularly useful to Sam, not only because I was a heavyweight, but because I could be plugged into any fight. That wasn't true of most blokes. A lot of fighters had plans and fears and whatnot, but I never cared who the guy across from me was. Short notice, no notice, notable, unheard of, whoever they were, we could throw down. That's how I ended up fighting Rony Sefo.

The fight was to be at the Mandalay Ballroom in Newmarket and, unbeknown to me, there was some tension between Sam and the Sefo boys. When Sam walked into the event – it was one the Sefos were promoting – Rony's brother Ray yelled at Sam to pay the cover. At the time Sam was a pledge for the Head Hunters, one of New Zealand's bigger gangs, but Ray wasn't going to take any shit from him at his own event. Sam told Ray he was happy to pay if Ray would accompany him to the toilets. As talented a fighter as Ray was (and still is), he wasn't that keen to go into a confined space with an angry Sam.

Rony was only a couple of years older than me, but he was much more advanced on his career path. He and Ray worked hard under Lolo Heimuli, and by the time I fought Rony they were already starting to make names for themselves internationally.

The guy Rony was supposed to be fighting had pulled out two days before the fight, so I got into the ring with about a day's notice. As soon as we touched gloves, I knew it might be a longer night than most of my other fights, not because I knew anything about Rony, but because he had abdominal muscles. I hadn't fought anyone with abs before.

Rony and I danced through six rounds, but the thing about Rony was that he just never tired, and he never dropped his hands – unlike most of the guys I'd fought up until that point. His chin never opened for business.

I lost that fight on points. I remember hoping I'd meet this bloke in the ring again, and vowed never to lose to the same person twice. Which is not to say that the close decision against a world-class fighter pushed me in my training, because it didn't.

Training then didn't mean to me what it does today. Today I train to win. Today I train to be not just the best fighter I can be, but the best fighter in the world. Back then training was just something to do. If there was something better to do, I'd be off in a flash.

At that time, though, I did start to realise how good I could be. Every so often, usually when training or fighting, a little squeaky voice of self-belief sounded off in my head.

You're the best fighter in the world, man; it's just that no one else knows about it yet.

I honestly used to hear that in my head. If I ever listened to that voice, however, it would be followed by a booming dissenting opinion.

Where did you come from? You think you can be shit? Just shut up, have another drink.

Living at Sam's gym taught me some of the basics of civilised independent living, and a little bit about working and budgeting, but it was never planned to be a permanent spot, so after about nine months with Sam I moved into Dave's parents' garage in South Auckland. I had a good little set-up there, with a bed, PlayStation, TV and VHS, and I remember it was on that video player that I got my first peek into the scale and spectacle of K-1.

VHS copies of high-quality kickboxing matches were a hot commodity around the gym, but no tape was as highly prized as the first-ever K-1 Grand Prix tournament. For those who don't know, K-1 was where mixed martial arts really began. Created by Kazuyoshi Ishii – the

Japanese karate master who started the Seidokaikan style of full-contact karate – the early K-1 tournaments were Japanese-only affairs, where local fighters would pit themselves in full-contact matches under traditional rules in front of tiny crowds. Soon these karate students were testing themselves against kung fu fighters and the rules were relaxed to create a more even playing field. As the rules became more permissive, Ishii-san found that his open style of karate was starting to mirror the styles of some of the European kickboxing champions.

In 1993, with the help of a group of Japanese businessmen (some with pretty colourful backgrounds) the organisation planned a one-off, eight-man invitational tournament in one of Japan's biggest indoor stadiums, so they could test their champion, legendary Japanese karateka Masaaki Satake, against the best fighters from around the world.

Fighters from the US, Croatia, the Netherlands and Thailand were invited to compete for the million-dollar prize, with the European kickboxers ultimately dominating. In fact, the only European fighter to lose – Ernesto Hoost – would do so in the final, against Croatian Branko Cikatić.

What was planned to be a one-off event turned into one of the most successful and enduring professional martial arts organisations in history, and the Europeans continued to prevail. In fact, of the nineteen K-1 Grand Prix events, only once has a non-European won. And that bloke spent a good part of 1993 sitting around in Dave's garage, smoking, drinking and watching VHS tapes of the K-1.

I'd never seen anything like the spectacle of K-1 before: the crazy production values, the giant crowds and the huge amounts of prize money. It seemed galaxies away from South Auckland.

'Shit man, that could be you,' Dave said to me while we watched Branko Cikatić, the inaugural winner of the tournament, beat up Satake in the semifinal.

It seemed a crazy, unwarranted statement, but part of me knew Dave was right. What was happening outside the ring was foreign to me, but what was happening inside the ring was as familiar as breathing. A scrap was a scrap, and I never, ever thought I would be out of my depth in one of those. Even then, having only ever slugged it out on the streets and in the clubs and halls of the North Island – and with a few losses too – I'd never thought any man in the world was a better fighter than me. No man in New Zealand, no man in Japan, no man in Europe.

The fight ended when Cikatić caught Satake with a left hook that knocked the giant Japanese fighter out cold. When the streamers waved and the flags started to fly, I turned to Dave and told him that I, too, thought I could win that tournament. It's very likely that I had a beer in one hand and a cig in the other, however, there and then, I believed I could win that thing. As was my way, though, as soon as the idea occurred to me, it disappeared again. It was an absurd thought, and the loud negative voice returned.

You're an uneducated street thug who came from shit, is shit, and will always be wading through shit. Have another beer, and another ciggie.

I probably did.

While I lived in that garage, I put myself in a rut I thought I deserved. During the day I worked as a lackey at a furniture factory called John Young Manufacturing, and at night I did door work at K'Rock, one of the roughest bars in Auckland. I started an irregular routine of extreme monotony and boredom at my day job and booze, drugs and scraps at my night job. Video games and infrequent training filled in the rest of my time.

As the months went by, a couple of possible futures emerged. The first came into focus one night when, while working at K'Rock, I was approached by a dude I immediately clocked as a little bit shady. I know what you're thinking. You're thinking, 'Where does a guy like you get off thinking that anyone else looks a little bit shady?' That's because you're thinking about this in binary terms – shady and not shady. Where I was from, there was a whole spectrum of shady and I wasn't even nearly at the bad end of it.

The guy's name was Tai – a big fella with tattoos bursting out of his collar and onto his face and neck. I knew these tatts meant gangs.

'I heard you can handle yourself bro,' Tai said to me.

I didn't tell him I couldn't.

'I've got some work for you if you want it.'

'What kind of work?'

'Collections work, man. People owe me money. You go and get the money. Real easy shit. You think about it.'

I did think about it. I'd spurned that gang life once because I assumed another, better life would emerge. It hadn't. Once again, though, I realised I didn't want what this dude was selling. What he was suggesting was a life that wasn't just peppered with fights, but real beat-downs and probably even worse than that.

That wasn't me. I didn't want to terrorise people. I had, and I felt shitty about it. I told Tai I was right where I was.

At my day job I saw my other future, which was perhaps even more unpalatable. One of my supervisors at the factory was a broken-down old Pakeha man, whose only energy for life was what he could muster from the office supply of powdered coffee. I disliked him because I saw in him a possible future version of myself. Every day I went to that place, a voice in my head got louder and louder.

You're going to be that old man. It'll happen in a minute, bro, in a second. You'll look up one day and you'll be him.

These were the two possible futures I saw in front of me, and I didn't want either of them. For whatever reason, though, I couldn't do anything to carve out a third path. I was in a rut and when my life hits a rut, the bad voices of those lesser angels start taking over. I found myself sporadically street fighting and robbing again, but this time it felt different. It wasn't a lark anymore. I was doing it because I was angry, and even though I hated myself for doing it, I couldn't seem to stop it.

Of course I ended up going down again for assault. This time it was just a month stint, but that month at The Rock (Mount Eden Corrections Facility) felt like years. We were in lockdown 22 hours a day and I soon started to despair. The last time I'd been in prison I was escaping my family home, escaping the old man. This time I wasn't escaping anything and there wasn't really anything to look forward to when I got out, either.

This was the first time it occurred to me that maybe I wasn't going to be anything more than a thug and a criminal. Maybe I should just embrace that shit, nom up and be done with it.

'At risk', I guess you would have called it. When I got out of the joint the second time, you could have pointed me anywhere and I would have followed. Luckily for the good people of Auckland, someone ended up pointing me towards Australia.

The idea first came into my head when my mate Tokoa, whom we called Tooks – a feisty little fella from school Dave and I had spent quite a bit of time with since – came home after a year in Australia. He first came to us before he left. We were sitting in Dave's garage playing Mortal Kombat on the PlayStation, and he told us about his plans across the ditch, and what he'd heard about Oz.

'All you need to do in Australia is just nod at the girls on the bus, and you're in. It's that easy there, bro,' Tooks said.

I didn't know about that, sounded like bullshit. Then Tooks came back, and he found us still playing Mortal Kombat. A year had passed and he'd come home to see his family. He found us in the exact same spot, doing the exact same thing. I was still bouncing, still at John Young Manufacturing. Nothing had changed.

When Tooks asked what we'd been doing, Dave and I gave embarrassed looks.

'Shit boys, you got to do something with your lives. You can't just sit around in a garage playing video games forever.'

He was right. It'd be pretty easy to spend another year the way we had the previous one and, before you knew it, those years would add up.

'Hey, was it true about the girls on the bus?' I asked Tooks.

'Come and find out.'

It was an idea, but not one that took form until Dave got a call a few months later. We were once again in Dave's garage, once again with PlayStation controllers in our hands, bashing away at a game of Mortal Kombat. When the phone rang and Dave picked it up, I could tell he wanted to get off the phone until he started to warm to what was being said. Soon he was quite animated and his attention moved to me.

'Mark. Hunt. My mate, you remember him?' he asked the person on the phone. There were a few words on the other end of the line, and Dave smiled. 'I dunno. I'll ask him. Hey man,' he called over to me. 'You want to move to Australia, live with my brother?'

I'd never been to Australia. I'd never been anywhere, except the country towns where Sam had taken me and the boys to surf, smoke weed and fight. I'd heard a lot about Australia, of course – not that different from NZ, but a little bigger, a little busier and with a few more opportunities.

It wasn't here, that was the main attraction of the place. What would I be leaving behind? Dead-end jobs? Clubs I'd been to a thousand times? Endless games of Mortal Kombat in Dave's garage?

I would be leaving one thing behind, though: a daughter. My daughter was born just after I got out of prison the first time. She wasn't the product of a committed relationship, she came from a couple of kids who were starting to grow into their bodies. When the girl's mother said she didn't want me to have anything to do with the baby, I was relieved. Some people could have handled the responsibility at that age, but I was a dangerous teenager who would have brought nothing to that kid's life besides misery and violence.

I was still a child myself then, and became something even worse than that – a broken, immature adult. I knew what it was like trying to grow up in a house with a broken, immature adult in charge. I knew the damage that could do.

Maybe this is all emotional retrofitting, but given who I was at the time it probably worked best for all involved.

It would have gnawed at most men, knowing their daughter was being raised by someone else. It did gnaw at me later on in life, but in that period I had no issue completely freezing out parts of my life that I didn't want to think about.

One day before leaving for Oz, a semi-naked man rode past me on a bicycle with his arms flailing, screaming obscenities. It took me a minute or so to even realise it was my brother Steve. When I recognised him, I felt no compassion or pity, just embarrassment. I wanted Steve to get the fuck out of my sight so I didn't have to think about him anymore. When the opportunity to go to Australia came, I did have to reach out to John, though.

Dave had a place for us to stay when we got to Australia; his brother George was willing to let us crash with him for a little while. We also reckoned we'd be able to get some door work as soon as we touched down, but the issue with our plan was getting there. We didn't have two dollars to rub together between us for the flights.

Of all my siblings, John was the one I'd had the most problems with because we were so different, and that was why I had to reach out to him. He was quiet and studious, and he saved his money. I didn't know how he was going to react when I asked him for cash. I thought there was a distinct possibility he would have a go at me.

Anger was one thing John and I had in common. My anger ran in ebbs and flows, though. My anger you could see build and recede. John's would lie dormant until, in an instant, the world was all fire and brimstone.

In the end I didn't even really have to sell it to him. He just nodded and told me he'd sort it out. No 'why', no caveats, just that he'd sort it out. He took a student loan to help us and it was enough money for both of us to get to Sydney, as I couldn't go anywhere without Dave.

Up to that point there had been scant occasions in my life when someone had done something for me without expecting a little bit of kickback later on down the track. I think John helped me because he knew how far behind I was when I started this life. I think John helped me because he was my brother.

None of us Hunts got much out of our family, but I got this, and it's something I'll always remember. I'd fucked John over, I'd helped send him to prison and had never atoned for it, but he was still there for me when I needed him. Such opportunities are worth their weight in gold. Such opportunities are to be respected.

Do you think I respected the opportunity? Fuck no. The first chance I had, I did my best to screw it up. In fact we weren't even out of the airport before I almost fucked it all up.

Chapter 5

SYDNEY, AUSTRALIA
1997

Dave and I were moving to Australia with one suitcase each and almost completely barren wallets. With no idea when the next chance for a piss-up might be, we decided to get stuck into the free booze that we were happy to find on the plane. By the time we touched down at Kingsford Smith Airport we were well pissed up. George met us at the airport and when he saw the state of us country cousins (not to mention the smell, which he did many times) he was not pleased.

George started giving us a serve before we'd even finished with the 'hellos'. Dave told his brother to settle those lips of his and I thought it was all a bit of a laugh until George turned to us and said, 'Do you two fellas want to kiss the floor?'

'What the fuck did you say to me?' I barked at George.

My fists were already starting to ball. I don't let people threaten me – it doesn't matter who you are or what you're doing for me. I still have problems letting that shit go.

'Keep that up and you boys will be living on the fucking street,' George said.

'Bro, it's not like we just took a bus to Otahuhu,' Dave said to me quietly. 'Let's just try keep it a little bit cool, yeah?'

He was right of course. We weren't even out of Sydney Airport yet and I was one drunken punch away from being homeless and probably arrested. I figured Australians would take a fairly dim view of drunken Kiwis punching on in their international airports. Not the best way to start my new life.

A couple of nights later, Dave and I met up with some other Kiwi fellas we knew and at the end of the night we had door jobs lined up. I had a red-hot go at fucking that up, too.

My first shift was at a place in Quakers Hill where the junior bouncers also had to collect glasses. I didn't mind that at all, as I had no delusions any job was below my station. Late in my shift I walked past one of the Aussie bouncers – an older guy who'd been hazing me and giving me shit all night. He stuck his foot out in front of me, causing me to drop a whole tray of glasses in a spectacle that brought every eye in the place on me. The other bouncers laughed, along with the punters and a lot of the girls.

I was straight back at school. I was in a place I couldn't just walk away from, with everyone laughing at me. The old fire in me started to flame, with the hair on the back of my knuckles beginning to tingle.

I cleaned up the broken glass then told the Aussie bouncer I wanted to have a quick chat with him outside. Pretty much as soon as we walked out the door he was lying on the ground with a shattered jaw. As I stood over him I didn't feel strong or exultant, I just felt depressed. This was another opportunity I'd fucked up, which is not to say I was repentant. I didn't see how this thing could have gone any other way.

I was told to go to the office to meet one of the bosses, but I figured I'd be meeting the cops there so I took off. When someone finally found me, it was the boss I was supposed to meet. He told me the bouncer I slugged had been hazing new guys for a while and they weren't unhappy with the situation.

The Aussie bouncer quit when he heard I wasn't punished, and I was given more and more work. I worked all across Sydney, in clubs and bars from the outer west to Kings Cross. I also picked up a lot of work at RSLs, and there I developed a very Australian habit, later to become a very Australian addiction.

Over the years I've lost hundreds and hundreds of thousands of dollars to the pokies, maybe even more, not to mention losing my mind from time to time. I took to poker machines like a duck to water. I was a kid in a new town, with few friends, no family and a lot of time on my hands. I'm not sure if you can draw a straight line between that feeling of escape I got when I first played video games as a kid, and me slumped on a pokie, pissing away my rent money, but both were similarly seductive.

I don't know, pokies just made sense to me, like video games had. I understood the parameters. I felt at home when I sat down. The difference between the two, though, was that I could usually stop playing video games when I wanted to. When I was playing video games, if I got hungry, I would eat, thirsty, I would drink; if I got tired, I stopped. That wasn't the case with the pokies.

I used to think I liked the pokies, but I know now I never liked them. I mean, how could I really like them? They never did anything for me except waste my time and empty my pockets. I don't know, maybe I did like them at the beginning, but after a few weeks I was just addicted.

Addiction is like a type of current that runs through your body, juicing you up, giving you a buzz, an energy. Energy you end up really loving. The only issue is, this current can't run under its own power, it can only run from energy stolen from other parts of your life. That all seems okay at the time – take a little from here, a little from there – everything's still running fine.

Don't worry about it. Everything else will work itself out. You might tell yourself that your addiction is starting to fuck with your life. You're drinking a bit too much, smoking too much, it's costing you too much coin. You might say you'll be paring that shit back – you might even mean it in that moment – but you'll be back. It's easy to get angry with an addiction, but it's pretty hard to stay angry with one. Then, pretty soon, it's rent day.

I managed to keep up the gigs working doors, but the pokies meant I rarely kept up with the rent. After a few months George got sick of my broke ass and told his brother to kick me out. I had no place to go. I told Dave that, but his hands were tied. I understood; I was a shitty friend. It wasn't like Dave and his bro were flush with cash either, and someone had to get money to the landlord.

I left George's place with all that I owned in a bag across my shoulder, and wondered what would happen next. I walked to the local shops and, while people walked past me, I thought about how there was cash in the pockets of every one of those fuckers. There was also cash in every store. If I wanted it, I could just go and grab it.

I looked at an Indian man in his curry shop, stirring some bain-maries of food. I could be in and out of that shop in a flash, and there'd be money in my pockets. I'd been there before and I could easily go there again.

What the fuck did this guy mean to me? I realised then that he did mean something. Not a lot – I wasn't yet well practised in the whole empathy thing – but he meant something. He did, and so did all those people walking past. They didn't deserve me.

I stuck my hands into my pockets and felt coins – two of them. Turns out I wasn't completely broke: I still had two twenty-cent coins.

I could see a phone booth. I picked up the receiver . . . who to call? I couldn't think of anyone. I picked up the *White Pages*, opening it somewhere in the middle, where I found a listing for a halfway house. I phoned them before I knew what I was going to say. It was an Indian dude who answered.

'Do you have any beds?'

'Yes we do.'

'I don't have any money but . . . I really need a place to stay. I can give you the money in a week . . .'

Of course he is going to tell me to go fuck myself. Of course he is.

'You can give it in one week?'

'Yeah man, yeah. A week.'

That was true, or at least it would be true if I could avoid chucking my wages into the pokies before getting them to this guy. He gave me the address and told me to come round when I could.

It was a good moment for me, a learning moment. I know no one ever deserves a medal for just deciding *not* to rob someone, but you have your battles, and I have mine.

I moved around a lot in my first couple of years in Sydney, usually leaving a rent debt in my wake, until I found some digs that suited my station and budget. I'd lived in some shitholes, but this particular place took the urinal cake. A dilapidated, falling-down old warren of peeling paint, suspicious stains and nocturnal noises, the place on Chalmers Street in Surry Hills was almost exclusively populated by junkies, except for me and Dave, who I shared a room with.

There were a lot of cons about living at that place, but the absolute worst thing about it was that even the junkies managed to move on. Not Dave and me, though.

It was while I was living there that I first went back to New Zealand. I thought a trip home might clear my head and give me some relief from the pokies. While I did manage to keep away from gambling while I was there, the old demons returned to haunt me.

I went back to see the girl I'd had a child with – not to see my baby, but for more sex. I drank and smoked, and even did P (crystal meth), which was becoming as popular as rugby in Auckland.

I hit the clubs, places where I used to scrap. On the last night of my trip, my fists flew again, which nearly got me back at The Rock for a long-ass stretch.

We were coming out of a club in South Auckland when it happened. I can't remember if it was closing time because I was pretty fucked-up by then, but that sounds about right. I remember jostling and shouting – the type that usually fringed a scrap – and I remember surging forward. It had been a while since I'd been in a scrap, and soon I was balls-deep in one. I copped one on the chin then retaliated, and then some. There were a lot of bodies in this fight – maybe dozens – so there was no shortage of people ready to throw their fist at me. When they did, I gave it to them.

The last guy who fronted me was a Pakeha dude. He didn't hit me, but tried to put me in an armlock. He got the same the rest did. As he fell to the ground, a shitload of police came into view and it seemed that all of them were running for me. As it turned out, a few plain-clothed cops had arrived on the scene to break up the fight, and one of them now lay on the ground doing an inventory of his teeth.

They cuffed me and put me in the back of a car with the cop I'd slugged. As we drove to the lock-up, he relished peppering me with gut punches.

'You like that, nigger?' he said as he was getting into my ribs.

'Come on bro. You can't just pop up on a brother like that,' I told him. This only made him angrier and wound him up a little more on the punches. I didn't blame him at all. I probably would have done the exact same thing if I were a copper.

After I was processed and chucked in a cell, I sat there stewing. *What the hell was wrong with me?* It wasn't like the old days before I left for Australia. Then I didn't give a shit what I did, I just acted on impulse, not caring in the slightest about the repercussions. I thought I was done with this stuff, though. Unlike the two previous instances, I really feared another stint in a Kiwi jail.

For the first time in my life I woke up in a cell feeling repentant. When I was called to court, I spoke sincerely with my state-appointed lawyer about how I was trying to mend my ways, and that all I wanted to do was get on my flight, get back to Australia, and stay right.

When that story was related – via my lawyer – to the judge I was amused to find it sounded exactly like the bullshit I'd spouted in court in previous years. What could I add, that I really meant it now?

The judge spared me, but probably not because he believed my story.

'When is your flight Mr Hunt?' he asked.

'This afternoon, Sir.'

'Do you promise to be on that flight?' he asked.

'Hundred per cent.'

'OK, you can be Australia's problem. I'm giving you two years, suspended, but if I ever see you again, you're doing every single day. I don't care what happens in Australia, but if you turn up in a New Zealand court again, you're doing the years. You hear me? Years.'

I thanked the judge, and I meant it. Going straight from the courthouse to the airport, I flew back to Sydney. I felt relief when I touched down. I'd acted like a maniac again in Auckland, but I'd gotten away without any consequences.

Turns out, though, that wasn't the case. I wouldn't know for some time, but I was going to be a dad again, a son this time, with the mother being the same girl as last time. I wouldn't meet him for a few years, but I would fall in love with Caleb, as I have with all my kids, and I'd do anything for him. He'd take my name, and he'd be my son and my mate, and he'd even help me out in my UFC fights. That time was still a few years away, though.

When I got back to Sydney, I realised I needed work that wasn't ten feet from a row of pokies or with blokes who wanted me to commit armed robberies with them. I pared back my bouncing shifts and took a gig sandblasting, which was easy work but could turn your arms and mind to mush if you did it for too long. The bulk of that sandblasting money still ended up being pissed away on pokies, but I'd like to think the intent meant something.

The big change that would end up shifting my life's trajectory altogether wasn't a change of work, but a change of recreation. While we'd been in Sydney Dave had become a big fella. Huge. The guy wasn't small when we arrived in Australia, but by the time I came back from New Zealand he was enormous. Unless he made some radical changes, he was going to be 200 kilograms pretty soon.

A Kiwi mate of his – a bloke called Denver Matthews – started getting stuck into Dave. He explained to Dave, in no uncertain terms, that he was becoming a giant waste of space. That was no way to live this life and Dave owed it to himself to change things. Denver was no angel, but he was right. If Dave wanted to make a change in his life, Denver said he was happy to help.

'How are you going to do that?' Dave asked.

'Well, if you're going to be a waste of space, you might as well be a waste of less space,' Denver said.

Denver suggested Dave should head down to Tony Mundine's gym, where he was training as a kickboxer. This sounded like it could work for me too. I'd really enjoyed training with Sam, and I thought perhaps a little bit of gym structure could do me good.

Dave and I started a routine, getting up most mornings at dawn, regardless of what had gone on the night before, rolling into the gym and getting in at least an hour's work to start pretty much every day.

These morning workouts felt good. They also reminded me how much I enjoyed the slap and snap of a fist or foot hitting the bag with power. As I started to get fitter and better, I'd recall that K-1 video, and I'd start to see Hoost or Cikatić at the end of those strikes.

I wasn't planning on doing anything more in Tony's gym than keeping myself fit and entertained until, one day, Alex Tui, a guy who worked there noticed me. He was a Tongan in an Aboriginal suburb whom, to this day, you'll still find at the gym morning and night. He told me he thought I could be a world-beater in the fight game. I wouldn't believe him until we were in a Japanese stadium, with tens of thousands of fight fans cheering for the latest K-1 acquisition, 'Marko Hunto'.

Chapter 6

SYDNEY, AUSTRALIA
2001

Mark took a big kick from Nathan [Briggs] . . . POP, flush on the jaw.
Most fighters would be hurt, or angry or scared, but it didn't even
register on him. He wasn't flustered at all; it was as though it hadn't
even happened. That's when I knew Mark could be very, very special.

LOLO HEIMULI (TRAINER)

They were happy mornings, at the Mundine gym. When
I'd arrive in Redfern, the suburb would be cold, dark and
silent, but while I pounded away at one of the faded old
heavy bags, sweat dropping onto the parquet floor, the
sun would start to fill the large windows and I'd hear the
sounds of the suburb waking. That place got me going.

Tony Mundine bought it in 1984, the year he retired
from a long boxing career. Tony's idea was that his gym

could be a centre for the inner-city community, not just Aboriginal people – of whom there were plenty nearby as it was smack-bang in the middle of an Aboriginal housing area known as The Block – but people of all races who could benefit from a good workout and the discipline required to stand against another man or woman with your hands raised. His idea wasn't a million miles away from what Sam Marsters was doing.

Tony Mundine is a legend in Australian boxing circles, but I only knew him as the old man of Anthony 'Choc' Mundine, a league player of rare speed and style who used to train alongside me, and who was about to start his own professional fighting career.

I went to Tony's gym not because of its pedigree, but because it was close, it was easy and cheap – no contracts, no addresses, no premium memberships, it was just a dollar a session, and even when I didn't have a dollar they'd never turn me away. I also liked it because it was often peppered with Islanders. I always felt more comfortable when there were other Islanders around.

An Islander who was almost always in that place was Alex Tui, a small, wiry, softly spoken man who'd managed the place since the eighties, and still does to this day. You'd never know unless you got him talking – which is no small feat – that Alex is an Australian kickboxing pioneer. One of the first Australasian fighters to train and compete in Thailand, he held a World Kickboxing Association world title, and, by sheer fate, was the cousin of Lolo Heimuli, the man who'd trained the Sefo and Auimatagi boys back in Auckland.

Alex says pretty much the first time he saw me working out he wanted to get me in the ring and testing myself, but he knew if he'd come on strong, he would have lost me. The only other gym I'd really trained in was Sam's, and for the first few months I barely talked to a soul. It also took me a while to feel comfortable with Alex.

He soon moved me over to sparring, which brought out the competitor in me again. I started working hard at the gym, but that's where my discipline ended – I smoked a pack of cigarettes a day (a habit that would extend past my K-1 GP win), drank thirstily and regularly, and my worst pokie-addiction days were still ahead of me. At least I had the gym, though. At least I had my morning routine, which required some discipline, some self-belief.

A few blokes at the gym suggested I take on a fight, but I just didn't see the point. As far as I was concerned, I was done with the fighting thing, until one day Denver said he had a fight for me which would earn me a hundred bucks cash in hand. I was down for that.

'Fight's in three days though, bro,' Denver said. Someone had dropped out of a bout and the organisers needed someone to fill in. The short notice meant nothing to me.

The day of the fight, I'd been sandblasting all day. The boys and I met at Central Station to take the train to the Serbian Club in Bonnyrigg, and we arrived just in time for my fight. I was starving – I wanted to get some Maccas before the fight but I was skint, so I rolled into the ring with an empty stomach, heavy arms and a headache.

I got dropped in that fight – the first time in my career – but my opponent, whose name and face now escapes me, couldn't finish me. I eventually finished with a points loss. I forced myself to have a meal straight after getting the cash in my hand, because while that money was in my pocket, I'd hear whispering in my ear, telling me where the nearest poker machine was.

When I spoke to Denver again he told me the promoters had contacted him about me fighting again, not because I'd shown that much aptitude, but because I'd shown I'd fight anyone, at any time, and I would probably last the rounds.

The next time Denver organised a fight for me I had time to train, and did a little bit. I slept the night before and ate beforehand. I don't remember much about that fight either, except that I managed to break my opponent's tibia with a leg kick.

After that, I got my first manager. A middle-aged Islander woman with a broad and ready smile, Lucy Tui (no relation to Alex) is one of those rare women who's perfectly comfortable wandering into a testosterone-drenched gym like Mundine's, and start hollering about what she'd found.

'Oh, you got yourself another heavyweight, Alex?' she said loudly while Alex was padding for me.

'Rolled in off the street, did he? You lucky bugger!' she boomed. She had her fingerprints on all aspects of organised kickboxing in Sydney; she promoted events, sat on federation committees, judged fights and managed fighters.

It had been a couple of months since my last fight and Lucy had been trying to find me, but I could still be a pretty infrequent visitor to the gym. After training, she took me out for coffee and told me she wanted to organise some fights for me. She said she wanted to arrange a path for me in kickboxing, if I was keen for it. She thought that if she could put me in front of the right people, eventually she could get me on some big cards.

I didn't get to do much talking that morning, but I do remember telling Lucy I wasn't planning on sticking around fighting for long. She wouldn't take no for an answer, saying that my last fight had given me some Oceania

amateur title – even though I'd taken a couple of hundred
bucks for it – and she wanted me to defend it.

I told her okay, quietly and without any weight to the
word. I quite often agreed to things I had no intention of
doing, just to end a conversation. This wasn't a 'no yes' or
a 'yes yes'. It was just an 'I want to go home yes'.

Shortly after meeting Lucy Tui, I met another incredible
woman. In fact, the most incredible woman I've ever met.
Lucy changed my career, but this woman changed my life.
I honestly have no idea who, what or where I'd be without her.

I met her at a reggae club I was bouncing at in Surry
Hills. The place was hazy with weed smoke, and the
rumbling bass danced empty beer glasses around the tables
closest to the speakers. I first saw her at some distance,
and I couldn't believe my eyes. I did a double take. My
first thought was that I'd seen an angel. She was glowing,
this girl. Sitting in one of the few illuminated spots in the
club, her pale skin and red hair stuck out in a joint full of
Africans and Polynesians, and she didn't seem to be real.

I walked past a few more times and when I saw her
laughing I realised that she was, in fact, a human being,
but that made her all the more desirable. Soon my eyes
wouldn't focus on anything else. I know it's corny stuff,
but if it's ever happened to you, you know how it works.

I grew agitated. *What if she left? What if this girl left, and never came back?*

Approaching girls was never my style. I'm a pretty shy person even now, but I was much more withdrawn then. When I asked this girl if I could sit next to her, there were klaxons blaring in my spinning head and all the moisture in my mouth suddenly disappeared. I don't remember a lot of what we spoke about – I got her name, Julie, and that she was a hairdresser from Western Sydney – but I remember the feeling of that conversation; it was so easy. I didn't want the night to end.

We arranged to see each other again, but our second meeting wasn't so sublime. We met up with a few of her friends, and I brought a mate of mine whom even I considered a little rough around the edges. I was nervous. I wasn't so practised at being in mixed company and I was pretty bad at polite conversation.

I drank a little too much that night and barely spoke to Julie. As she got into a cab, I knew I'd ruined things and, frustrated and pent up, I hurled a pie I'd bought at her taxi. As the meat and pastry hit the back window, Julie and I both thought the same thing. *Well, that was that.*

Only it wasn't. I do believe in fate, in no small part because I bumped into Julie again a few weeks later, at a bar neither of us had ever been to. I look around my house and see the kids now and the life behind me, and marvel at my good fortune.

Things were easy again that night, with the conversation flowing and I started to have feelings I'd never felt in my life before. We arranged a date, just the two of us, and then another and another. The more I saw her, the more I wanted to see her, and soon she was spending a lot of time in Surry Hills in the flophouse, where I now had my own room.

Julie wasn't scared off by that place or my rough mates, nor how I was suspiciously and perpetually skint. She just wanted my company and that confused me a little bit, but I'd take it. We never really had to do anything together, either; we were happy just lying on my bed talking. We'd talk about anything and everything, sometimes smoking a bit of weed to mute the world outside.

One day I got talking about my childhood, my family and my old man. I'd not spoken to anyone about that shit before – not my mates, or even John, Steve or Victoria. I'd never really thought about how I felt or acknowledged to myself how thoroughly fucked-up it all was. I'd spent years just trying to get away from it, but when I started telling Julie about it, I tried to dredge up every rotten detail. It was as though something had been sitting on my lungs for years and now I was coughing it all up.

I didn't know how badly I'd needed to tell someone until it all started pouring out of my mouth. Victoria spoke to people about what had happened, and now I had. John and Steve didn't, and I think that's why they've suffered the way they have.

As I spent more time with Julie, I realised how far behind I was in some of the most basic life skills. One day she asked me when I'd last washed my sheets. I told her I'd never washed them. I had no idea that you had to; we never had in my house. I was also awful around Julie's friends. I smoked and drank and simply couldn't stop gambling, but she stuck around nonetheless. She became my tether to a civilised life.

The more time I spent with Julie, the more I felt that quiet assurance that there was going to be something for me in this life, that one day I was going to be great at something. I didn't know what it was going to be, but there'd be something. Late one night, I told Julie that, both of us lying in a haze of weed smoke. She said she knew.

After I met Julie, I spent less and less time at the gym, until one day Denver caught up with me and told me he had a fight for me, a boxing bout in Bondi. The fight was paying a couple of hundred bucks, so I was in.

The fight was at Bondi Diggers, a nice joint on the top of a hill with views down to the iconic beach and off across the ocean. When I got to the venue, I found that my fight was one of the last on the card, so I set myself up with the boys at a table near the ring and got stuck into the booze and smokes.

When they said my name, I got into my shorts and into the ring, where I found John Wyborn, a lanky boxer from Grafton, across from me. I muddled my way through the fight and when the decision was rendered and it was announced that it was Wyborn's fight, I didn't much care. Win or lose, I was getting some cash that I could use to take Julie out.

A little after that fight, Lucy found me and took me out for another coffee. 'Barry Raff told me that you took a boxing bout on one of his cards. Is that right, Mark?' she asked.

I nodded.

'Why the bloody hell did you do that? That was a sanctioned fight. You're a pro now. That title defence I was trying to arrange is stuffed now.'

I told Lucy I needed the money.

'If you need money, just let me know, I'll arrange some work setting up chairs for my shows or something, just don't take any more bloody fights until I can arrange them for you, okay?'

I agreed, but Lucy probably knew that my word would only hold for so long so she arranged another fight for me pretty quickly. I took that fight with a few days' notice, up on the Gold Coast, against Nathan Briggs.

When I got to the venue it was full of bikies and rednecks, and as I walked out to the ring they were baying for my blood. I was this Kiwi coconut, facing off against a good old Queensland boy with a strong local fighting pedigree.

Cornering for Nathan was his twin brother, Paul, a kickboxing world champion, his father, David, a trainer and ex-fighter, and a few other tattooed brawlers. Alex couldn't make the trip up, so I was cornered by Lolo, Lucy and a female bantamweight fighter Lolo had been training.

I was out-struck from the first bell. A tall and talented fighter, Nathan kicked the shit out of my legs, and when I couldn't move much anymore, I started taking flush shin shots to the head. The crowd loved it – they were getting exactly what they paid for. Between the third and fourth rounds, Lolo stressed that I had to change things up. I asked what exactly he had in mind.

'I . . . don't know,' he said. Not something a fighter ever wants to hear between rounds. 'You're going to have to do something else,' he yelled as we walked back into the middle.

That round continued like the others before them: with me standing in front of Briggs, having my legs and head battered. When we got into a clinch, I could hear Lolo's voice in my head. *Something else, something else . . .*

CRACK.

I'd wound up and thrown an elbow across Nathan's temple, which was equally satisfying and illegal. This was a kickboxing fight, not a *Muay Thai* fight, and elbow strikes were outside of the rules.

Soon the ring was flooded with people, with the Briggs corner jumping in first, then mine, followed by a few pissed-up punters. Almost single-handedly Lolo, using his exceptional standing and calm demeanour, managed to cool the situation down without any unsanctioned blows, and even got the fight started again. I lost, but I've never forgotten how cool Lolo managed to stay in the heat of those circumstances. This would stand me in good stead when the two of us got to the UFC.

Unbeknown to me, I started to gain a reputation after that fight. Even though I wasn't winning, I couldn't be stopped and would agree to any fight. I was a promoter's dream. They started calling me the punching bag of Oceania.

My next fight was in Melbourne against Chris Chrisopoulides, a tall and powerful heavyweight. Once again I'd been called in as a replacement at very short notice – just 48 hours this time. When Lucy came to pick me up from my place in Surry Hills the day before the fight, she could see and smell the night before on me.

'Well boy, at least you're not fighting today,' she said to me as I got into the cab.

After weighing in, passing my medical and getting some dinner, Lucy and I got back to our hotel at around 9 pm. 'You're going to need your sleep. Nine am for breakfast?' she asked.

I nodded and went to my room. I looked at the bed – it looked pretty comfortable, what with its hospitality tuck and all, and I was exhausted, but I'd seen a bank of poker machines on my way in. *Maybe just a little flutter.*

Lucy had breakfast alone, until the hotel security guard approached her. 'I reckon your boy is going to get smashed,' he said.

'Oh yeah? Why's that?' she asked.

'He only just went to bed, and he's been drinking, smoking and playing the pokies all night.'

The phone woke me; it was the front desk telling me I had to check out. When I met Lucy downstairs she was not pleased.

'Don't worry. It's all going to be fine,' I told her.

She wasn't so sure. She wasn't sure when we got there and I had a chuck. She wasn't sure when the fight started and it looked like I was still asleep. She wasn't sure for the first five rounds, each of which I lost. She wasn't sure until halfway through the sixth round when a right uppercut of mine landed on the Greek's chin.

Since I was a kid I've always known when a punch of mine has found the spot, and before he started to lift off the canvas I knew it was all over. I had to walk past an unconscious Chris Chrisopoulides to get to my corner and Lucy.

'I reckon you thought I was going to lose,' I said. Turns out this fight was the most important of my career up until then.

The K-1 organisation had been steadily gaining momentum since the first Grand Prix I'd seen in 1993, and in 2000 it was going global. There were seventeen events planned around the world, with many serving as feeders for the bigger Japanese events, all culminating in the Grand Prix which was now happening at the 80,000 seat Tokyo Dome.

At that time the Seidokaikan master Ishii-san still sat atop the K-1 organisational tree, but he'd allowed others to control their own, local branches, and the man to be in control of Oceania would be proud Turkish–Australian ex-fighter Tarik Solak. By the time Tarik was granted the K-1 licence, he had a long history of mounting big events, including the one that had just hosted a hungover coconut who woke up just in time.

Lucy knew Tarik was planning to hold his first K-1 event – an Oceania championship – at the start of the next year, so she started getting into his ear. After all, what would an Oceania championship be without the region's punching bag? I was eventually invited to fill out the eight-man roster, and I'm sure it was because of my ability to stay in a fight, not because Tarik thought I had any chance of winning. To understand how he felt about my chances, you only had to look at the poster for the event, which featured me behind the other fighters, standing in the dark, barely visible.

I took one more fight before the championships against veteran Tongan heavyweight Neilson Taione, who was another of Lucy's fighters. This fight was supposed to be a K-1 warm-up for Neilson – her golden boy at the time – not for me. While I fought, though, Lucy and Lolo got a glimpse of the form I would find in the next couple of years.

Taione won a unanimous decision against me, but after the fight Lolo told Lucy the fighter she should be concentrating on was me. Compared with the other fighters I was unfit, undisciplined, inexperienced and far too old to be as unpolished as I was, but Lolo thought I could be a special fighter, if Lucy could ever get me to knuckle down.

I hadn't been knuckling down. After the Chrisopoulides fight I borrowed a couple of hundred bucks from Alex, which I fed straight into a pokie machine. With no means of repaying the cash, I stopped going to the gym.

After Alex told Lucy about my absence, she approached me with an offer of a sea change. She had a spare room at her place in the ocean-side suburb of Manly, and if I started training again with Alex she'd let me move in. She'd help arrange my timetable and make sure I didn't piss away this opportunity to fight at the Oceania K-1 event.

It all sounded pretty good – I liked Lucy and got a sense that she did care about me, and not just as an asset either – but I wouldn't commit to it. I didn't tell Lucy for some time that it was because I was embarrassed about the money I owed Alex. When I eventually told her, she did her big old belly laugh. 'Alex doesn't give a shit about that money. You think a guy like you walks into his gym every day?'

If Alex did care about the money he never gave me any indication of it; he just seemed happy I was back at the gym with him. Excited about the prospect of the tournament ahead, he immediately set out a training regimen that involved running and conditioning as well as technique training and sparring.

I never dreamed I'd do it, but I ended up completing all of it. My days suddenly became very full, starting with a run at 4.30 am and finishing at 10.30 pm with work, fitness training and a shitload of public transport in between.

Those pre-dawn runs became meditation for me. I enjoyed the quiet of the mornings, with the sound of my own breathing the only thing in my head until some thought formed, which would be studied from a hundred angles. I know it's silly, but for many of those runs the thought that would end up in my head was the 'Secret Sound'. During the day I was working at a company that made Blackmores vitamin pills, and we'd listen to a tinny radio locked onto a local FM station. There was constant promotion of a competition whereby, if you could figure out what was happening in the short sound grab, you could win $10,000.

That sound would play in my head over and over again, and I'd dream about what I'd do with the cash. It seemed so easy: just an A–B line between the cash and my pocket. The only other times there'd been such a straight line between me and a decent amount of cash had been when there was talk of committing some criminal act or other.

When my mind was clear and fresh, I'd wonder why the frick I was thinking about a radio contest. Then, during one run, it occurred to me that I wasn't thinking about the Secret Sound at all, I was thinking about the K-1 Oceania tournament. It also had a ten-grand first prize, and surely this tournament cash was closer to me than any radio contest money.

When I tell people I never really trained for a specific fight or goal until I was 25 years old, they don't believe me. In those early days I used to train because I felt like it, not because I was going anywhere with it. I'd never thought about anything but the day ahead until that point: it was as if next week was a possibility, not a certainty.

Things changed after that run. Soon the only free time I had was on the weekend, when Julie would come over from her parents' place in Campbelltown to me in Manly, and we'd spend full days in my room just talking, listening to music and watching movies. Did I have time for gambling and drinking? No – I managed to stay away from both in that little period before the K-1 Oceania Championships, and it was probably the happiest time of my life up until then.

I must have been running on the weekend sometimes too, because I remember coming back to Julie one morning after having my revelatory moment about the Secret Sound and the K-1. I told her I was going to win the Oceania tournament. I'd never said I was going to do something like that before; I'd often declared that I *could* do something, but had never said that I *would*.

She grunted and went back to sleep.

Chapter 7

SYDNEY, AUSTRALIA
2001

> Mark was a really shy, very humble guy, and he was
> always underestimated in the way a lot of Polynesian
> fighters often are. He was a little roly-poly, and perhaps
> a little short, but you'd underestimate Mark at your own
> peril. He had a lot of power, which served him well,
> but it was his resilience that made him great.
>
> **PETER GRAHAM, TRAINING PARTNER AND K-1 AND MMA VETERAN**

It wasn't Alex Tui who taught me how to fight, or Sam
Marsters, or Lolo, or anyone. Those guys taught me about
ring craft, technique and discipline but, really, I knew how
to fight before I met any of them. Most of the guys in the
UFC started in another martial arts discipline – in Brazilian
Jiu-Jitsu, or *Muay Thai*, or freestyle wrestling, or karate,

or *Vale Tudo* – and then later picked up the rest of the skills needed to be a mixed martial artist.

When you get into the UFC Octagon, announcer Bruce Buffer says what your base skill is. When I'm announced, he says I'm a kickboxer, but that's not exactly true. My style was already set when I started K-1, before I'd even stepped foot in a gym. No matter how many fights I have left in me, I'll never have more fights in the ring and Octagon than I did on the streets of Auckland, where I really learned to fight.

This man is a South Auckland Scrapper . . . That's what Bruce should say.

My trainers drill me now according to what I'm likely to face when I get into the Octagon, and give me some specific responses and attacks that will be useful, but when I step into that cage I don't go in with the mental clutter most fighters have. MMA has become a very strategically deep sport and every day it becomes more so, but thankfully you can still win if you can punch the other guy until he can't continue, and that's always my plan.

I go into my fights now with the same strategy I had when someone would throw me that look in the mid-nineties – I go in there looking to get that big shot. If I do, it's all going to be over. The only thing I need is an empty head, and I can let my fists go. After the Oceania tournament, I knew how I could empty my head. I had to train.

When I've done the work for a fight, I can't wait to get into that cage. In the cage, I'm free, like a greyhound running or a bird in flight. In the cage I can do what I'm best at, what I'm built for. When I'm fighting, I can transcend my life and feel grace. If you're in the ring with me and my mind is free, God goes through my fists. If God be with me, then who can be with you?

I flew down to Melbourne for the K-1 Oceania tournament well rested, well trained and well and truly ready to lay some people out. Despite my record indicating it should be a short trip (it was a 'loser goes home' tournament), I knew for the first time in my career that I'd done the work and, with the work done, I just didn't see how any of the other fighters could stop me.

My first two opponents gave me the opportunity to settle some old scores. In the quarterfinal I was drawn against Clay Auimatagi, the same guy who, with his brother, had come at me with chains and bats in South Auckland so many years ago. There was no talk of this between us before I knocked his ass out of that tournament, nor after. I have nor had any ill-will.

In the semifinal I was drawn against Rony Sefo. With his brother absent, already an established K-1 fighter earning the big bucks in Japan, Rony was the tournament favourite. I hadn't really thought about my loss against him in Newmarket back in the day until I saw him in Melbourne, and it made my skin crawl. I was hoping our paths in the tournament would line up and when they did, I couldn't wait to get in there. I'd done plenty of shit in my life I wished had gone down another way, and a lot of that was irredeemable. Not fighting, though. If you lost a fight, you always had the opportunity for a rematch and when I stepped into the ring with Rony, I resolved never to lose one of those.

Rony is another good guy I have no ill-will towards, but at the time he was another bloke who really needed to get his ass beaten. I fought within myself against Rony, picking my spots with a cool dispassion that won me a unanimous decision.

In the last fight of the tournament I fought Phil Fagan, a muscular British fighter who'd resettled in Australia. I accounted for him easily, laying him out cold in the second round. When all the tournament brass piled into the ring to give me accolades and a trophy, it seemed I was the only one who wasn't surprised about how the day had played out. Lucy seemed to be the most astonished of all, and also the most ecstatic.

'I hope you've got a bloody passport,' she said.

'I didn't swim to Australia.'

Did I need my passport to pick up my money? It seemed an odd thing for her to say. 'What do I need my passport for?' I asked.

'You're going to Japan, boy.'

Someone had probably told me at some point that if I won the tournament I'd be going to Japan to fight in one of the big K-1 events feeding the Grand Prix but, as a rank outsider, it's also possible no one had thought it necessary. Either way, I never took the information on board. Even after Lucy told me, it didn't seem real.

'Oh yeah, okay,' I said blankly.

Travelling to Japan? It was like someone had informed me they were going to triangulate the hypotenuse of my pancreas. It didn't mean anything to me. After I won, I just concentrated on the here and now, which by the way was pretty fucking good.

I'd cruised through that tournament like a hot knife through butter, and Tarik Solak congratulated me warmly after the fight. It was very different from my last post-fight interaction with the bloke when, after the Chrisopoulides fight, Lucy had approached him about the fighter's meal money. He'd looked at her as if she'd asked him to lick her armpits. He eventually reached into a wad of cash and threw two 50-dollar notes onto the ground in front of the two of us. In that moment I should have learned a little about the relationship between management and fighters, but I didn't and would have to learn about it later, the hard way.

Julie and I were happy homebodies, so I spent the ten-grand prize money on my room – new sheets, a new TV, a new DVD player, some kung fu movies and some new duds. I felt like a king in that room, and could scarcely believe that I could treat my girl to a night out of Chinese food and drinks, before heading back to fresh sheets and a DVD copy of *Bloodsport*. I kept up my training, too, not because I was thinking about Japan, but because I was enjoying the routine of life.

After my Oceania win some other first-class kickboxers gravitated to the Mundine gym, so I soon had a couple of tough heavyweights to spar against: Peter Graham, a local guy who would carve out his own solid K-1 and MMA career; and Auckland Auimatagi, Clay's brother.

Peter, Auckland and I went hard in the gym. One day it would look like Peter had it over me; the next day Auckland would be on top; and then maybe me the day after that. I loved those battles, and they brought out the competitor in me.

I trained intensively for my first trip to Japan, which is not to say I was ready for it – I wasn't. I was ready for the fight, but I wasn't ready for the experience. The fight was to be in Nagoya, a mid-sized port city, against Jérôme Le Banner, a very experienced Frenchman known as the best fighter on the K-1 roster to have never won the Grand Prix. He'd won everything else and had got through all the way to the Grand Prix final, but had never made it over the last peak.

Everything about that trip was overwhelming. I've been to Japan dozens of times now and I love the place – the people, the food, their passion for combat sports and especially how they've embraced me as an athlete – but when I flew to Nagoya that first time, I was a kid in an adult's body, a stranger in a strange land. Lucy and Alex had both travelled in Asia before: Lucy had been to the K-1 as an observer and Alex had fought around the world, but I'd only been to Australia and New Zealand, which have only the slightest of cultural differences.

Merely checking in to the hotel – something I'd done maybe three or four times in my life – was over-awing. K-1 was a behemoth of Japanese television then, and even at feeder events like the one in which I was competing, the lobby was packed with an army of journalists, cameramen, groupies and functionaries, not to mention the fighters and their considerable entourages. It wouldn't take long for me to get my gaggle of hangers-on and good-time boys, but in Nagoya it was just Alex, Lucy and me. I felt as though we'd arrived at a party we'd been invited to by accident.

Like every K-1 event I've attended in Japan, the Nagoya event organisers had thought of everything a seasoned fighter could possibly wish for. The thing is, though, I wasn't a seasoned fighter. I'd only ever trained in the Mundine gym or with Sam, and now I was being asked to train in luxurious ballrooms in front of the European beasts of the sport, whose disparaging eyes darted when I wandered in with my Tongan corners.

I wasn't used to Japanese food, either. I ate a lot of noodles in Sydney – usually the cheapest meal around, and a noodle restaurant in Surry Hills was my date-night spot of preference with Julie – but these Japanese noodles were unfamiliar and, for me, unpalatable. I barely ate while I was there.

I hated the media obligations, too. I wasn't a confident speaker. What did I have to say about Samoa? About my background and my life? Nothing. I had nothing to say. How did I feel? How did I *feel*? What the hell did that even mean? Shit, when I checked in to my room I couldn't even figure out which toilet to piss in.

For most of the week Alex and Lucy were nowhere to be found, they were out, sightseeing and whatnot, and I was lonely in a way I hadn't been since I was a kid. I was a million miles from home and Julie. Everything outside the hotel was confusing and everything inside was, too.

I flicked on the TV looking for something familiar and comforting. Now having been on countless Japanese TV shows, I still don't understand them, and as I surfed through the channels in Nagoya I only found pure confusion until, with great relief, I found something I could take in. It was *Doragon Bôru Zetto* or as I knew it, *Dragon Ball Z*. This show was all about the scraps, not the dialogue, so my enjoyment didn't depend on an understanding of the language the characters were speaking. It was nice to sit down and understand what was going on.

I went into my fight against Le Banner hungry, meek and, in the first and last time of my career, with a sense of trepidation. I'd only seen these famous K-1 fighters on VHS, and had certainly never been in a ring with one. I half-expected them to be superhuman, like Goku in *Dragon Ball Z* or Ryu in *Street Fighter 2*, and I hadn't discounted the possibility that Le Banner might be about to *hadouken* me from across the ring

When I was called from backstage I stepped into a stadium, a big one – the 40,000-seat Nagoya Dome – in which every seat was filled with a bum. It was too much; the week had been too much, the stadium was too much. Then when the announcer said the Japanese version of my name

– MARKO HUNTO – it felt surreal in an uncomfortable way. I just wanted to get this thing over and done with and get back on the plane.

At the end of the first round Jérôme got me in the corner and started throwing undefended bombs, a couple of which landed flush. The crowd bayed, the shots kept coming, Jérôme had the finisher's look in his eyes . . . but I was fine. I was fine.

The bell rang and as I walked back to the corner it occurred to me this prick didn't even hit that hard – I'd been hit harder than this my whole life. I even managed to drop the dude in the second round with a running leg kick, but as the last seconds of the third and final round ticked away I knew I'd lost on points. In those moments one thought spun around my head over and over again. *That was it?* The guy couldn't throw fireballs from his hands or Dragon-Punch twelve feet into the sky or do anything I couldn't do. If that's all those guys had, I could get my hands on them. If I could get my hands on them, I could certainly put them to sleep. They weren't the characters from *Dragon Ball Z*, and Jérôme wasn't Super Saiyan. I was. I was the super SAMOAN.

When I walked into the Nagoya Dome I didn't want that fight. When I walked out of it I desperately wanted to do it all over again. I wanted to go back in time half an hour with the knowledge that it was just men in this ring, not supermen. I really wanted Le Banner again. I wanted that guy again, I wanted to knock his fucking head off, and I wanted it to happen now. Even though I'd been cowed and overwhelmed by my Japanese experience, it had made me realise that I could make a career in fighting. I could beat Le Banner, no doubt whatsoever. I would beat Le Banner.

For my first-round exit of that tournament I earned US$27,000, which meant I could cut down my hours at the factory and concentrate more heavily on my fighting. When I arrived in Sydney I went back to training straight away, but things had changed. I still loved working with Alex, but I realised that my needs were going to outgrow Lucy's capabilities pretty quickly. As much as I appreciated what she'd done for me, I wondered whether she really understood the Japanese fight game.

One day at home I picked up the landline phone, to find it dead. When I asked Lucy what was going on, she said I was welcome to pay the phone bill if I wanted to. I was annoyed because I paid rent at that place, which as far as I knew also covered expenses. I figured it was time to move on.

Whether by chance or by design, one day Lucy brought Hape Ngaronoa, a kickboxing instructor who had opened a gym in Western Sydney, around to her place, and as soon as I met the guy he started wooing me, saying that I should move and train with him.

I liked the guy. He was a Kiwi and we knew a lot of people in common. He played chess, like I did, and I liked his aggressive attitude and shoot-for-the-stars mentality. He told me there wasn't anything I couldn't do, and I was starting to believe that. He said I just needed the right help.

The clincher was when he offered to help me with renting an apartment in Liverpool. Julie was a Western Sydney girl, and I immediately took up Hape's offer. We could get a place of our own in a part of the world in which I'd always felt comfortable. Surry Hills and Manly had their charms, but Western Sydney always felt like home: a place full of good, hardworking people with no pretensions, who wouldn't thumb their nose when a tattooed Samoan kickboxer walked past.

By the time I went round to look at the place Hape had suggested, I was already sold. I knew I wouldn't have any problems telling Lucy – her life was pretty full and she probably felt relieved when I said I was moving out of her home and had found a new manager. But it wouldn't be so easy to tell Alex.

Alex and Lucy came as a team, so if I was quitting Lucy I was also quitting Alex. Alex was a guy I loved, and he'd only ever done right by me, but I felt I needed a change in my corner, too. Alex was a nice guy and would never be anything but. Hape had the dog in him and I knew he would put the dog in me too. I couldn't have any timidity in my corner if I was going to stand up to Jérôme and his ilk.

When I told Alex, he shook my hand and wished me luck. He meant it, too, there's no doubting that. He knew it was going to be a big year for me, and all he'd ever wanted was for me to reach my potential. I did feel a twinge of sadness when I started training with Hape, but he quickly barked me into shape.

I trained my ass off in his gym, but for some reason I couldn't get another fight scheduled. I started to wonder why. Hape said that after my last few fights, I was no longer seen as the region's punching bag, but a guy who could take your head off and root your record.

After a few weeks at his gym, Hape brought another guy into my team, a slick, fast-talking Pakeha Kiwi whom Hape said was going to be my manager. I don't ever remember agreeing to having Dixon McIver as my manager, but I had no problem with it. The guy could talk the hind leg off a donkey, and had managed both Rony and Ray in the K-1. It seemed to me that he knew what he was doing. What a poor judge of character I ended up being.

Dixon told me he'd heard another major K-1 event was going to be held in Melbourne. As part of an attempt to extend the K-1 brand, their biggest-name contract fighters would be fighting outside Japan. The rumours started to become facts. The best guys were coming to Australia for an event at Rod Laver Arena, then Melbourne's largest indoor stadium.

There was a spot for a local fighter, too, who could gain entry by going through the second K-1 Oceania tournament, which now would give thirty grand to the winner. The way I trained for that tournament and the attitude Hape instilled in me, there was not one motherfucker who would be able to stop me.

My first fight was against Nathan Briggs, and I've already explained how I felt about rematches. I knocked him out in the first minute of the fight. My semifinal was against Andrew Peck, a powerhouse Kiwi fighter who'd been discovered by Sam Marsters in similar circumstances to mine. Peck had been on a run of knockouts, including Rony Sefo and Auckland Auimatagi, but I laid him out even more quickly than I did Briggs. I went into the final of that tournament against Peter Graham having about a minute and a half of fight time.

I'd trained with Peter at the Mundine gym for some months so I knew what a talented and proud fighter he was, but after chipping away for two rounds he presented a spot, like Andrew and Nathan had before him, and I finished him off in the third round. I was once again the champion of Oceania, on a fast track to the first major international K-1 event in Australia.

There were three months between the Oceania championships and the K-1 event, and I should have spent that time training. Instead I ended up loitering around New Zealand. The plan, which was arranged by Hape, was to jump across there for one or two appearances before coming back and knuckling down in preparation for the Melbourne event, but a few days became a week and then another, and then a few more, with us going down the line to Napier.

Soon after we arrived in Auckland it was clear that coming home with a bit of cash was not good for me. I enjoyed spending time with the boys in Auckland – I revelled in the role as a returned hero – but with them it was easy to slide back into the lax morality of my teenage years. I wasn't hauled up in front of the judge whom I promised I would stay Australia's problem, but there was drinking and smoking and drugs, then, a few months later, I went so far off the rails I couldn't even see them anymore. When I finally turned up in Melbourne I'd piled on an extra nine kilograms and my gas tank was considerably smaller than it had been.

Travelling on a shuttle with the rest of the fighters heading to the venue, I heard Ernesto Hoost say loudly that he was going to kill the 'Aussie boy' in the tournament. I remember being glad I wasn't an Aussie. At that time Hoost, nicknamed 'Mr Perfect', had a winning record of 81–16, having taken pretty much every major kickboxing title, and he was reigning K-1 Grand Prix champion.

Now I know he was, of course, talking about (and to) me. Later that day there was a press call, including a group photograph. I was happy to be in with the rest of the seven big-name fighters, until a meaty paw deliberately and obviously reached over to obscure me from view when the photograph was taken. The message was clear: you're not one of us. I was back at primary school, with the capillaries in my face ready to burst. I looked along the arm and found it was attached to a big, eraser-headed Croatian named Mirko Filipović, who is now known as Mirko Cro Cop, a moniker he picked up due to his time in his country's elite anti-terror police unit.

I didn't mind what Hoost had said, he was just mucking around, but this Cro Cop slight meant something. It meant I was just a regional annoyance, not one of the big boys, not part of the group. I wanted to fix this fucker, and I was monumentally pissed off that I wasn't in any kind of shape to do it.

When I stepped into Rod Laver Arena I had my first taste of what fame would feel like. I'm sure few people in the crowd knew who I was, but they knew I was the local fighter and that was enough for them to get cheering. My first fight was against Japanese boxer Hiromi Amada – I caught him in the first round with a right hook and sent him to sleep. My semifinal was against Ernesto Hoost. While he didn't get to kill me, he did kill my legs, throwing what felt like endless inside and outside leg kicks that soon rendered me one big, lumbering punching bag. I took Hoost to a decision, but the match went to him.

After that I agreed to fight in an event in Auckland, but as far as I was concerned my year was done; I'd have to try to get those big boys of K-1 in 2002. As was the case the previous time, when I landed in Auckland I partied, even before the night of my fight. I was caught by Tarik coming in to the hotel at 3 am, having had a pretty substantial night.

The next day I wandered my way through three rounds against Peter Graham, watched the referee raise Pete's hand, patted him on the back and then headed straight for the ciggies and booze.

I was planning to get back into training, but not until the next year. In the meantime I had lined up a little sparring against Sydney fighter Adam Watt, who had qualified for an upcoming K-1 event in Fukuoka, the winner of which would gain entry into the big dance, the Grand Prix. I was a little unfit and slow and Adam fairly beat the crap out of me in those sparring sessions but I was happy to turn up; he was a good guy, if not sometimes a little volatile and temperamental.

I remember I was at a barbecue at Dave's house in Auburn, when I got the call. I had a beer in my hand and had just finished a ciggie, when the phone rang. It was Dixon.

'Mark, I've got some good news and some bad news. The good news is that Cro Cop has picked up an injury and can't fight in Fukuoka. I just got the call, and they want to slot you in, they want you fighting in three weeks.'

'The bad news?'

'The bad news is you'd be fighting Ray.'

Three weeks' notice against a guy like Ray Sefo would be no joke, but of course I said I'd take the fight. I'd never turned down a fight and I wasn't going to start now. Even though I may not have been able to win, I knew I could at least last the rounds. The Japanese fans would always appreciate that.

When the negotiations started, the K-1 started to nickel-and-dime me, trying to give me considerably less cash than I'd earned for my previous Japanese fight, and I started to wonder if I really wanted to take this fight after all. I was going to fight Ray Sefo, the undisputed king of the region, with whom I had my own personal history. Ray would be coming in as strong and fit as humanly possible. He desperately wanted to be the first man outside Europe to win the Grand Prix, and had lost in the final of the previous year's Grand Prix. With this being the last opportunity to qualify for the 2001 Grand Prix, he'd no doubt been red-lining his training.

It was actually Adam Watt who convinced me to go. 'What have you got to lose?' was the cut and thrust of his argument, and it was an argument that spoke to me.

Chapter 8

TOKYO, JAPAN
2001

It was good that a Samoan brother made it, and represented us. I was really happy for Mark. No, really, I was. I was happy, I am happy . . . wouldn't mind having another crack at him, though.

RAY SEFO, K-1 VETERAN AND PRESIDENT, WORLD SERIES OF FIGHTING

Sometime in 2001 the Japanese decided to adopt me as one of their dudes. Early in the year I had barely any profile in Japan – a K-1 0–1 nobody as far as the Japanese were concerned, if they were concerned at all. By the end of 2001 I was doing fast-food advertisements and presenting at the Japanese MTV Music Awards.

It all started with that fight against Ray. I'd gone over to fight him for a repechage tournament, one of the eight ways a fighter could qualify for the Grand Prix. My fight against Ray was a first-round fight so there wasn't much interest building up around it, but it's now remembered as one of the most famous fights in K-1 history. That fight was really my introduction to the broader fighting world.

Like I said, though, I went into that fight unfit, so my normal strategy of 'taking the other guy's head off' developed into 'taking the other guy's head off in the first minute of the fight'. Ray is, like me, a Samoan Kiwi, and our heads don't come off too easily.

I came out swinging, every punch a sidewinder. Ray looked a little shocked at my early output but weathered the storm like you would expect. At the end of the round I could tell he was enjoying the abandon of the contest. K-1 was big, serious business and most fights were very technical. But Ray seemed to like being in the ring with someone who was willing to stand there and trade leather with him.

The first round ended not only with the customary clapping, but also cheers from the Japanese crowd. I was told about the cheers later because all I could hear was my own breathing and the pounding of my heart. After a round of effort, I was rooted.

I went into the second round sucking up the big ones, and now out of ideas. I swung for some more home-run shots but the punches were flying past Ray's bobbing head.

As the seconds ticked by, my feet were getting heavier and heavier. I could punch, but I couldn't move much. Ray moved me around the ring, bouncing punches off me and every so often I'd load up a big right or left. A 2–1 combo landed right on his scone, with Ray nodding his approval. He was in it now. I was too.

Oh, we're in a scrap now, boy. The ring, the crowd, the city all started to fade away. Now it was just a couple of concrete-headed Samoan scrappers doing what we do best.

What have you got for me fella? Ray loaded up with a five-punch combination, finishing with a left hook that landed flush on my chin. Good punches, real good. He's got heavy hands, Ray.

When he was done I dropped my hands and stuck my face out towards him so his nose was right in front of mine.

'THAT IT?' I yelled.

Ray threw me a smile, moved in and kissed me on the cheek. It wasn't a 'fuck you' kiss, as some people have suggested, it was something else. We were brothers, man, a couple of Polynesian brothers tied to this moment we would both remember for the rest of our lives.

I patted him on the back and then loaded up with a 2–1–2 combo, with each punch landing flush. Ray rolled backwards and took them, all of them, before dancing a little dance with a huge grin on his face. I threw my arms out to my sides.

Okay boy, your turn. Think you can knock me down?

Ray danced forward and started throwing all he had. I dropped my hands, bit down on my mouth guard and let him rain down on me.

'YEEEEEESSSS,' I screamed at Ray while his fists flew into my head. After ten or so unguarded shots I started to shoot back and soon we were throwing in turns. When the bell rang and the punching stopped, the ring came back, and the crowd, and the context of the fight.

I looked out at the Japanese crowd and they were cheering and clapping, but they also had looks of disbelief. That's not how the European fighters do it, and certainly not how the Japanese fighters do it. It seemed many in the crowd didn't know how to react. There was laughter, which is not something you hear regularly at a Japanese combat sport event, and people with their hands on their heads, shocked.

South Auckland comes to Japan, eh?

When I was called for the third and final round, I was well and truly stuffed and I knew, no matter how conditioned Ray might have been, he must have been rooted too. We kept trading as best we could, but the fight had peaked and we got across the line with a lot of clinching and counter punching.

The crowd cheered when Ray took the decision, but I knew a good part of that appreciation was for me. I patted him on the back after the fight. That was some scrap. My tournament may be over and my Japanese record may now be 0–2, but it really was a scrap for the ages.

I'd only been backstage for a few minutes when I heard a bit of a commotion going on. I only vaguely noticed it; I had a towel hung over my head, trying to unring that bell Ray had struck. Then I heard my name.

'Hunto-san, Hunto-san?' It was two Japanese men – one I recognised as an organiser of the event and the other I assumed correctly was the fight doctor.

'Sefo-san, he can . . . he cannot continue. Can you continue?'

Always boy, always.

Ray's vision had been jarred by our exchange in the second round and he was unable to count how many fingers the doctor was holding up. The doctor had ruled him unfit to continue on to the next fight. When the doctor gave me the same test I passed with flying colours. Probably the first time I'd ever topped the class in a test of numeracy.

I had twenty minutes and I'd be moving on to the second fight, which would be against the winner of the fight between K-1 veteran South African Mike Bernardo and the bloke I'd been sparring with less than a month earlier, Adam Watt.

My fight with Ray had been a war, but Adam's with Mike was a beat-down. Bernardo fancied himself as a bit of a gangster and he and his entourage had been trying to intimidate Adam since we'd arrived in Japan, but it seemed the Aussie wouldn't be so easily flustered. Bernardo went down twice in the first round of their fight, before being finished after two and a half minutes.

Twenty or so minutes later, Adam and I were facing off. When the announcer introduced us and the ref gave us the rules I could still feel Ray's punches in my head, but as soon as the bell rang I was on again and ready to scrap. I still had slow feet, but fast hands. I took the middle of the ring, letting Adam dance around me while he threw a series of kicks and testing jabs. When he came into range I threw power punches and I dropped him a couple of times. I mostly managed to avoid the barrage of spinning attacks his camp must have thought I was susceptible to.

In the third round, with me ahead on points and my gas tank close to empty, Adam got me in a corner for one last attempt to get over the top of me. He threw combo after combo and mostly I had to just cover up, until I saw Adam dropping his right hand and shoulder when he threw his combinations. The first time I caught him with a left hook, the punch just glanced away. The second landed flush on the jaw. He dropped to the ground and the ref called time to have a look at a big cut I'd opened up on him earlier in the fight. That thing wasn't going to stop pissing blood, so they called it.

One more fight.

Adam's guys started congratulating me, then Hape and Dixon. Soon it dawned on me there weren't any more fights that day – I was done. This hadn't been an eight-man tournament as I'd thought, but a four-man one. I was heading to the K-1 Grand Prix – the final eight in the biggest martial arts competition in the world.

The next day I flew back to Tokyo and was taken to a soundstage in the Fuji TV building, where I found the seven fighters I'd be competing against in the Grand Prix, amid a large set. The tournament's draw was to be finalised live across Japan on prime-time TV. On set there were eight positions on an elevated stage – A–H, with the positions representing a spot in the draw. A and B would fight first, then C and D and so on. If you wanted to avoid fighting the person in position A, you could place yourself anywhere from E to H and it was guaranteed if you were to fight the person in position A, it would be in the final.

Each fighter drew one of eight balls, with each ball bearing a number. As luck would have it, Jérôme Le Banner got ball number one and chose position A. Of course he did. Le Banner was on a thirteen-fight undefeated streak and the heavy favourite for the tournament. Why wouldn't he consider himself the A-1 man?

I got ball number three. That meant I could essentially choose whom and where I wanted to fight. The inexperienced Danish fighter Nicholas Pettas had already picked a spot, across the draw from Jérôme, and I could tell people were expecting me to pick him. Pettas was the least heralded fighter on the bill (except for me, of course), but I knew exactly whom I wanted to face. I didn't want to risk someone else getting the opportunity to punch Jérôme's ticket.

The sound from the crowd grew louder and louder as I drew closer to position B, and claps and cheers when I gave the big Frenchman a bit of a shoulder shove and just a hint of the South Auckland stare. Jérôme clocked me with a look of disbelief.

Afterwards the Japanese media had quite a few questions.

'Did you understand how the draw worked?'

Yeah.

'Do you think you can beat Le Banner-san?'

Yeah.

'Do you think Sefo-san is upset?'

Nah.

'Do you like hamburgers?'

Yeah.

'Do you really think you can beat Le Banner-san?'

Yeah. In fact I'm knocking his ass out.

That night I went out in Tokyo with some of the other guys and got a little taste of what life would be like as a K-1 star. We travelled in limousines, drank expensive champagne and everywhere we went, they treated us like kings.

Ray met up with us too, and we ended up in a restaurant owned by a guy who would become a good friend of mine. Konishiki (born Sale Atisano'e) was another bloke with Samoan blood pumping around a big frame who'd been welcomed by Japanese sport fans. Born in Hawaii, Konishiki was discovered in Honolulu by a scout as a teenager and competed as a sumo wrestler from the age of eighteen, until his retirement fifteen years later. He'd reached the sumo rank of *Ozeki*, the first foreign fighter to achieve that rank, and at 287 kilograms Konishiki had been one of the heaviest and most popular sumo wrestlers of all time. He was a great help to me when it came to understanding the ins and outs of Japanese culture, and he's still a close friend today.

Konishiki took us all to a karaoke joint in Roppongi and while he sang (like an angel, might I add), Ray draped his arm over me and toasted me with a whole bottle of champagne.

'Welcome to the K-1, bro.'

I felt good. I felt great. I felt like I'd arrived.

We left that joint and headed for a nearby nightclub, but we were stopped by a group of pissed-up American sailors on shore leave. They started giving Ray shit about his clothes and it was obvious that they were looking for a scrap. With Ray and me were Stefan Leko, Jérôme and Mike Bernardo, and I'm now racking my brains trying to find a worse group of blokes to fuck with. Our days of street scrapping were behind us, though, so some of Ray's entourage took over and beat those guys up while the rest of us piled into the club, joking and laughing, into a roped-off area where bottles of champagne and a cordon of staring Japanese punters were waiting for us.

When I arrived home in Sydney, I got straight into training. One day Julie asked me what I was going to be earning for the Grand Prix. I knew it was the world's most lucrative martial arts tournament at the time, but I didn't know the details. When I asked Dixon what the breakdown would be, he went back to the contract and told me that my appearance fee would be what I'd earned for my last fight, which was $8000, and also any prize money. And what was the prize money for a first-round loss? Jack and shit.

'I'm sure I told you that,' Dixon said to me. This was the first little bump on a road that would lead to financial ruin. The only way I'd get paid was if I got past Le Banner, but that was fine by me. I was coming for the Frenchman's head, and nothing less.

I trained my ass off for that tournament (some of it, anyway). For the first time since I was thirteen, I stopped smoking and drinking. I was working towards something, which other people might do as a matter of course, but I hadn't lived my life like that.

I wanted Le Banner on a plate; I wanted it so badly. I had slow-motion dreams of my fists flying, steady and true, and Jérôme's eyes rolling backwards. I saw the man lying unconscious at my feet.

'You know, if you beat Le Banner, you can write your own cheque,' Dixon told me one day at training. The huge success of K-1 would inevitably spawn usurpers so the K-1 was bullishly protecting their assets with long, lucrative contracts. He reckoned I could get one of those if I beat Le Banner.

'You don't even need to win the tournament, you just need to take Jérôme out, and you'll become a commodity.

The Japanese like you, but now they need to respect you,' Dixon said.

I told him to chill. I got it.

When I arrived in Tokyo I couldn't have been more ready. I was fit, strong and relatively slim. I knew I had to stay cool until I got into the ring, though, which wasn't the easiest task. Unlike my previous visit, it seemed the whole of Tokyo knew about the upcoming tournament – with billboards and posters of us covering the city. Not just that, it felt like everyone knew who I was, and the story of how I'd picked Jérôme. This was obviously a narrative the K-1 had been selling in the lead-up to the tournament.

I tried to stay as focused as I could, and I managed it most of the time. I checked in to the luxurious Shinigawa Prince Hotel, which had been completely sequestered for the tournament. I brought friends with me this time, too – not just Hape and Dixon, but mates from back in the day, including my mate Tokoa, who'd pushed Dave and me to head to Australia.

My headspace was exactly where it needed to be when I got to Tokyo, and Hape had a lot to do with that. While Alex had the temperament of a Zen master, Hape was a more volcanic figure but excellent at directing his fury at my opponent.

'This fucking guy thinks he's better than you? He's been punched one too many times. You're going to eat this fucking guy up with chopsticks,' Hape barked while we trained in the ballroom of the Shinigawa Prince.

He was right. Fuckin' oath he was right.

In the pre-fight press conference, someone asked Jérôme what he would do if I stuck my chin out at him the way I had against Ray.

'I'll punch it off his face,' he said robotically. Nice guy, Jérôme, but man he has all the personality of Ivan Drago.

When I heard that I couldn't wait for the fight to start. I'd never wanted anything so much before. I can imagine the feeling was close to how other kids had felt on Christmas Eve. The knockout was already mine – the presents were already wrapped – but having to wait was torture.

As impressive as the UFC is as a billion-dollar global brand, it'll never match the grandeur and sense of occasion of the K-1 Grand Prix. When I was finally called into the Tokyo Dome for the fight, I stepped into a reality I'd never known before. I was on a stage that bore eight giant Roman columns, one of them emblazoned with my name. A huge picture of me sat above it and lasers flew around illuminating 80,000 cheering fight fans.

'From the notorious streets of South Auckland all the way to the Tokyo Dome, Mark "The Doctor" Huuuuuuuuunt!'

the American announcer called. Aussie kickboxing commentator Michael Schiavello had given me the nickname, suggesting I was someone who prescribes sleeping pills. I looked at my fists.

OK Jérôme, take two of these and call me when you wake up.

When my intro music started, I put all my concentration on suppressing the electric feeling starting to spread across my skin.

I looked straight ahead as Hape yelled this and that in my ear and barely acknowledged the crowd when I got into the ring, which was now flashing like something from the movie *Tron*. Hape had formulated a plan for the fight against Jérôme, but when the bell rang I promptly forgot what it was. I was there to do to him what I'd done to a hundred men before him. I was looking for the punch that was going to separate this man from his consciousness.

Jérôme probably out-scored me in the first round. He's a big guy, much bigger than me, and every time I tried to get into his range he'd fend me off with long jabs and head kicks. In the second round, though, I started to time his fends and got into his range. That's when I started throwing with abandon. The crowd roared when one of my wound-up uppercuts skied between us. I hadn't gotten him, but they were cheering for the unlikely narrative that the K-1 had been suggesting.

With a minute left in the round, Jérôme got me into a corner and started throwing combinations, getting me in the Thai plum, an allowed clinch in which taller fighters can quite often get heavy knees into a smaller fighter's head. He might have got me with a couple of knees, I can't remember. If he did I didn't care. We were into it now.

I caught him with a couple of counters and he backed off, out of the corner. Then I dropped my hands and stuck my chin out like I had with Ray.

Come get it boy. Come get it.

The crowd absolutely loved that, and it seemed Jérôme was put off by my showboating. The sound levels soared as he came at me, and soared again when I wheeled around and caught him with a flush straight right.

Le Banner retreated into the corner he'd just trapped me in, and there I threw one of the longest combinations of my career. A few of the fourteen or so punches glanced off his gloves, a few missed altogether, but most of them caught the big Frenchman, including the last two which snapped his head backwards as though someone had deleted his spine. Le Banner didn't so much fall to the floor, as splashed.

The place went bat-shit, but I managed to keep pretty cool. Hopefully I had two more fights and, besides, I'd already seen all this. As far as I was concerned, I'd won this fight weeks ago.

When I got backstage and into the training rooms, there was an unexpected intrusion. It was Tarik Solak, who bounded in energetically. I was confused, wondering what the hell he was doing there.

'Mate, I just got you forty grand,' he said.

'What for?' I asked.

'For the knockout. Call it a bonus. Forty grand, pretty good, huh?'

K-1 didn't offer any knockout bonuses that I knew about, but I'd happily take the cash. When I told Dixon about the money, I could tell he was pissed. Tarik's 'bonus' was another salvo in the long-simmering war between Solak and McIver over control of Oceanic kickboxing and specifically K-1 rights. Tarik had previously controlled all the big guns in that fight, but with the win over Le Banner, I had instantly become an arsenal, and Tarik wanted to try to get me in his camp. To Dixon's credit, though, he managed not to complain openly about the intrusion. After all, his man had a semifinal to fight.

Ernesto Hoost had managed to get a decision against lanky German–Croatian fighter Stefan Leko in the first fight of the tournament, so I was pretty happy at the prospect of avenging both my European losses in quick succession. Sadly, it wasn't to be. Hoost had sustained a leg injury in his fight, and with Bernardo, the reserve fighter, also injured, Leko would have to do.

My output in my second fight wasn't quite what it had been against Le Banner, but I did manage to drop Leko in both the first and second rounds, and that was enough to get me the unanimous decision and into the final fight. Twenty minutes later I was backstage wearing a Samoan lava-lava (sarong) around my waist, an asoa (lei) around my neck and a T-shirt that said 'Bad Coconut', waiting for a million-dollar fight. The prize money for second was almost a fifth of the first prize, reflecting the uniquely Japanese 'winner takes all' spirit of K-1.

No problem there. I never thought about anything except that number-one spot. I was given the gift, and I'd done the work. I wasn't going to be stopped.

Michael Buffer, one of the most recognisable voices in the world, cut through the hubbub of the crowd with his trademark intro. 'For the thousands in attendance, and millions around the world . . . LET'S GET READY TO RUUUUUUMBLE.'

I stepped into a cherry picker that had been brought in to transport me to the ring. A spotlight landed on me, and while an orchestral version of Queen's 'We Are the

Champions' played, I floated some 40 metres above the ground towards the ring.

On the other side of the stadium was Francisco Filho, a Kyokushin karate fighter from Brazil wearing a white *gi* and black belt. A life-long *karateka*, Francisco is one of the few men to have undertaken two 100-man *kumites*, in which the fighter endures 100 consecutive sparring rounds against similarly high-level opponents. This would be a fight between the *dojo* and the streets.

The fight wasn't the most exciting I'd ever been in. I tried to follow Hape's game-plan, which was to tortoise while I got close enough to the Brazilian's head, then take it off with my hooks, but Francisco did a good job of keeping me at bay with long, hidden karate head kicks, which are thrown with a bent leg and only obvious at the last moment.

In the final seconds of the third round I could feel the fight was not yet won so I bum-rushed the Brazilian with a flurry of punches and knees, trying to snatch the victory. Nothing really connected, and when I got to my corner I felt we might be looking at a draw.

We were called back into the middle of the ring and the refs announced their results. All three judges had seen the fight 30–30. We were going in for one more round.

As soon as I got back into the middle I could see fatigue in the face of the Brazilian fighter. I thought to myself that

I only had to work hard for another three minutes. Just 180 short seconds of punching and kicking and I'd be set. I'd be the baddest motherfucker on earth, with a million bucks in my pocket. I'd be set. Just one more frickin' round.

I took the middle of the ring early and kept it for almost the entire round. Cutting off an exhausted Filho a number of times, I delivered heavy body shots while he was trapped against the ropes. He got a couple of decent head shots off and a couple of jabs and a kick, but he couldn't stop me from coming at him. We were both completely rooted at the end of the fourth round, but I started to feel that I'd got there.

'Get ready for another one,' Dixon said when I went back to my corner, but I reckoned I'd done enough. I'd turned it on when it needed to be turned on, and I thought I'd won that last round purely because of my activity and effort.

When the ref took our hands I felt that winning feeling. Like the KO of Le Banner, the victory was already the truth even though it hadn't been declared yet. As the announcer started speaking in Japanese I began tapping my chest in celebration.

Then I heard the words 'MARKO HUNTO', and it was time to go bat-shit. I leapt around the ring; I did the running man; I hugged all and sundry. Tarik was in the ring, along with Dixon, Hape, Peter Graham and Adam

Watt, and also Ray. He hugged me with genuine warmth, but I could also tell he was hurting. I'd snatched what he'd been working towards for so long and from his hands, no less. This was my moment, though, not Ray's.

Kazuyoshi Ishii grabbed me and kissed my forehead. He was as happy as anyone in that ring. My Cinderella journey from obscurity to the Oceania tournament, to the Repechage B tournament, and now to the peak of combat sports, it was completely unprecedented. That was something he could sell.

A podium was set up and while I stood in the middle of it, I watched Tarik and Dixon jostle for a position next to me. As is the Japanese way, I was festooned with victorious totem after victorious totem – a silk sash, a giant medal, a golden cup and a crown. It felt like I'd just beaten the final boss in a Spacey and they were powering my character up. Then they produced the totem I really wanted, that giant cheque.

I didn't really take it all in then. In fact, it only really struck me a few days later when I walked, barefoot, onto my flight back to Australia. As I was settling into my business-class seat, one of the flight attendants came over and asked if I had any shoes. I didn't. I'd only taken one pair of shoes with me to Japan, and I'd given them to a guy on the street after celebrating.

'Okay, let's see what we can do,' she said with a smile.

An Aussie guy across the way called over to me. 'Hey, champ. I've never seen a millionaire without shoes before,' he said, raising his champagne glass to me. 'Congratulations.'

Holy shit, I AM a millionaire!

I might have been a millionaire, but I was also still that renegade kid from South Auckland. I'd managed to stave off my vices for a couple of months in the lead-up to this tournament but, with the job done, I succumbed to them all, and then some.

I wouldn't stay a millionaire for long. That's the thing about shoeless millionaires – they're usually targeted pretty quickly by someone selling shoes . . . and the rest.

Chapter 9

AUCKLAND, NEW ZEALAND
2002

I spent a few days in Japan after my Grand Prix win before flying home, and those days would speak of what the rest of my Japanese martial arts career would be like. After my win at the Dome I was taken to a private dining room in the hotel to sit down with the K-1 brass and talk about my future in the organisation. When the functionary came backstage to give me the invitation I was told in no uncertain terms Dixon would not be joining us.

'We started this thing together, we're going to keep going together,' Dixon kept saying as soon as he heard what was going on. 'We're a team. It's you and me, bro. You and me.'

He was pretty much pleading in the end, but none of it was necessary. I didn't think we were a team, but I do think you should dance with the girl you came with.

'Don't worry, man,' I said to him. 'I'm not going to fuck you.'

When I arrived for the dinner, the maître d' bowed deeply then led me through a quiet restaurant of wood-panelling and dim lighting to the private dining room. Inside, Ishii-san and his lieutenants sat with Tarik, awaiting my arrival. There were brief congratulations, and sake, then we quickly got onto the reason Ishii-san had summoned me.

'Mark, we want you to be managed by Tarik. We know him. He is a friend of ours. We don't know this Dixon.'

I told them I couldn't do that. I knew Tarik was an astute businessman and he obviously had a great working relationship with Ishii-san and the K-1, but I just didn't trust the bloke. When I saw him in that restaurant, all I could think about was him throwing those notes on the ground in front of Lucy and me as though they were scraps for a dog.

A year after my K-1 win, I was seated next to Tarik on a flight heading back to Australia from Japan, and he asked again if I would sign with him.

'You and I, we both came from the streets, Mark. We understand each other. Why don't you work with me?' Tarik asked.

At that point I was pretty jack of Dixon's shit, but I told Tarik why I wouldn't sign with him then, and why I didn't after my Grand Prix win.

'Do you remember when you threw money at Lucy and me at the Oceania championship?' He didn't. 'That's why I'm not going with you.'

'Mark, please go with Tarik,' Ishii-san said to me. 'It would be in your best interests, trust me. You have signed nothing. You can go with Tarik very easily,' he said.

That was all true, but my team was my team and I'd given Dixon my word. I knew very little about Japan and Japanese culture, but I did know one thing that might speak to the Japanese men.

'Mr Ishii, I know you're trying to look out for my interests, but I gave Dixon my word. I can't break my word.'

They weren't happy, but that was the end of the conversation. The next day, Dixon sat down with Ken Imai, Kazuyoshi Ishii's right-hand man, to hammer out my contract. I really only got one decent concession out of those negotiations – that I would be bound to K-1 for two years, not the five they wanted – but I now know the money was verging on insulting.

K-1 was one of the hottest properties on Japanese TV; tens of millions had watched me win the Grand Prix and I was the new champion, but I ended up signing for US$60,000 a fight.

'Is this the best contract I can get?' I asked Dixon after he presented it to me.

'Mark, that's as good as it gets.'

I'm not sure what happened with that contract. Maybe the K-1 were still trying to get me to deal with Tarik, or maybe Dixon never had a chance of getting any more than that, but either way I left hundreds of thousands of dollars on the table that day – maybe even millions – but I signed anyway. I was still being paid US$60,000 a fight, which was twice as much as most people I knew earned in a year, and I'd just won the biggest single cash payout in kickboxing history. I thought I'd never have to think about money again.

With the contract signed, I had two public appearances to make before I could head home. The first was a photo op with Royce Gracie, the Brazilian *Jiu-Jitsu* scion who had won the first four UFC events.

The UFC was first conceived by Californian ad man Art Davie, screenwriter John Milius and Rorion Gracie, Royce's brother and eldest son of Hélio Gracie, the originator of Brazilian *Jiu-Jitsu*. The idea came to Art Davie after he saw some Gracie family videos, in which it was claimed that their martial art, BJJ, could be overwhelmingly effective against any other martial art discipline, be it boxing, kickboxing, kung fu, *tae kwon do*, wrestling or *savate*. Davie proposed an eight-man, full-contact tournament to test that claim. When the Gracie family were brought on board, Rorion chose Royce, the skinniest of the brothers, for the tournament, purportedly because it would look more impressive when the Brazilian finished off the other, much larger fighters.

Royce and the Gracie family had become synonymous with mixed martial arts, with their style of fighting spreading to Japan in 1997 when Rickson Gracie, another of Hélio's sons, fought famed Japanese wrestler Nobuhiko Takada in the first Pride Fighting Championship, which took place in front of 50,000 people at the Tokyo Dome.

By 2001, K-1 and Pride shared space on the Fuji TV roster, so there I was, being rear-naked choked by a smiling Royce in front of a wall of laughing journalists and flashing cameras. I hated being choked like that, just like I'd hated being grappled into submission by Sam Marsters. The feeling of powerlessness took me back to the house in South Auckland and the overpowering control of the man of the house.

I was more enthusiastic about my second obligation – an ad for Maccas. I don't know whether they'd arranged the ad because it was me who had taken the Grand Prix and not one of the calorie-counting Euro supermen who normally won, but the Japanese lapped up the image of me with a giant tray of hamburgers and a goofy, excited look on my face.

With all those burgers under my nose, I started to feel the old hunger. I hadn't exactly lived monastically in the lead-up to the Grand Prix, but I'd limited my vices in a way I never had before, and wouldn't again until I got to the UFC.

After a short stop in Australia and a few nice, quiet dinners with Julie, I flew to Auckland and went fairly nuts. I was young, rich and ready to party. In Japan I'd become an instant celebrity, with crowds forming as I walked down the street, but in Australia and New Zealand no one besides a small group of dedicated fans knew who I was. I was free to do whatever the hell I wanted.

During that trip to Auckland I mostly lived in hotels; I even had a stint at the penthouse at the Carlton Hotel. I had good times up there, holding court with my mates, racking up on the baby grand piano, before telling the concierge we needed a car to get back down to South Auckland so we could hit the clubs.

Some of my mates were in the same rut I'd left them in, but some had found changes of fortune. My return to NZ coincided with the rise of a new drug that would rot Kiwi brains and teeth for the next decade, which was locally known as P but better known around the world as crystal methamphetamine, or ice. A sugary-looking amphetamine which, when smoked, gives a high that makes cocaine feel like drip coffee, P was starting to bring in serious boom times for some of the shadier characters in Auckland, including a couple of mates of mine – Tommy, an industrious street-level dealer who was working his way up in the drug game, and Porter, who was happy where he was and carried a shitty-looking thirty-eight revolver. As he'd slap it on the counter at the penthouse we'd make endless jokes about it.

'Bro, the only person in danger with that gun is you. Just sell it and hire Mark. Much more efficient, much more intimidating,' Tommy said once.

'He can't afford me,' I said.

One night we went to one of my favourite joints down south, a place called Shakers. With an almost exclusively Polynesian crowd, the club was heaving with punters shaking to all the old favourites – Dr Dre, Snoop, Boyz II Men, Aaliyah, Mary J Blige and then . . . my jam – the LL Cool J song that I'd had playing while I walked into the Tokyo Dome.

I thought about the journey I'd made from Auckland to Sydney to Tokyo. I thought about where I was and where I'd come from. I had a drink. I thought about my family. I had another drink. I thought about my family. I drank some more. I thought about that house, just a short jog from the club, and that old fucking bastard. Then I hit

Tommy up for some P and enjoyed the rest of the night, footloose and care-fucking-free.

In the morning, I drove south to where Mum and Dad were living. They were renting a dingy, sparsely appointed apartment, but at least they had a VHS so we could watch my Grand Prix fights. Dad kept pausing the video to point out everything I was doing wrong. I shouldn't have been dropping my hands. I shouldn't have stood toe-to-toe with Ray. I really shouldn't have been smiling in the ring. Every time he pressed the pause button it felt like I was going back in time.

I wanted my parents out of my head. I thought perhaps I'd be able to do that by fulfilling my obligations as a son with some cash, so I'd buy them a place where they could fuck off and leave me alone. My old man pretty much laughed at the first few apartments we viewed. Those places were a vast improvement on what they were then living in, but none of them were good enough. Soon it became apparent that they were only going to accept a house. I went to an estate agent and described what I needed: a nice, stand-alone place with a garden and enough bedrooms for other family members if they needed a place to live. When we found a spot that ticked all the boxes, my parents were still less than impressed. After looking around the place my old man only had one thing to say. 'Where's the second floor?'

In Samoan culture there is an obligation to look after your parents as best you can when you grow older and have your own means. In my mind that obligation had been battling with the memories of beatings and rape, but I thought with the purchase of the house I could put the whole mess somewhere over there, inaccessible from the regular mental paths and passages of my everyday life.

I bought the place in cash. I thought I'd done what I had to do. My parents had never had anything in their life, and now I was buying them a loan-free house, a palace compared to where they'd been living. That would do.

As I drove away, I thought that my dad could stay there and rot – which he eventually did – away from me, away from my thoughts and memories. I felt angry and proud, but also sad and belittled. I was a boy again. I was destroyed.

I'm excellent at compartmentalising my life – banishing any thoughts or memories I choose not to have – but it turned out I couldn't just wash my hands of my dad like that. That bastard was like rotten fish in that regard.

I'd dumped a pile of cash out of my newly bulked-up bank account, and it had given me no real pleasure. I attacked the rest of that money with gusto. If anyone wanted to eat, we ate like sumos; if anyone wanted to drink, the first few dozen rounds were on me. I was also open to business propositions.

I'd been given a Jeep Wrangler after the win, but when one of my friends was trying to shift a late-model BMW I bought it in cash. Dixon tried to remind me that I didn't need to own two luxury vehicles in a city I didn't live in, but everything worked itself out when I ended up totalling the Jeep. I left it on the side of the road and went on with my life.

I was a man on a tear. I was in a city that, as a young man, had offered only small channels to live my life in – but now the whole horizon was open to me. I was, once again, susceptible to suggestion.

One of those suggestions was from Tommy, asking if I'd like to buy some P. Not a small, usable amount – a large, sellable amount. Tommy suggested that if I could get twenty grand together, he could help me turn it into sixty grand in a few weeks.

Obviously I didn't need money, but I wasn't saying no to very much at the time, so I said, 'Fuck it, let's do it. Let's sell some crystal meth.'

Thankfully I never ended up selling any of the P. Any decent drug dealer knows you don't get high on your own supply, but I wasn't going to be any decent drug dealer.

I had plenty to do at night but little to do during the day, so one morning I started smoking the P, then walked over to the Sky City Casino and sat down at the highest stakes pokie machine I could find. For the next three days my ass rarely left that seat. I took a break only to piss and get stuck back into my giant bag of meth.

I spent twenty grand on the first day, regularly sending my mates off to get more sheaves of cash so I could cram the notes into the mouth of that beast. I blew twenty grand on the second day, too, and by then I was a dribbling automaton, existing just to press that button, over and over and over, and in one drug-buzzed haze I'd pissed away a yearly salary for most of my mates, ending up in the pockets of who-the-hell-knows. On that second day I became obsessed by the jackpot – a slowly increasing number illuminated above the row of machines where I was sitting.

On the third day, a few times my fortunes danced up to the line of success, before retreating and taking with them thousands more dollars. In the afternoon, with at least another twenty grand invested, I won – possibly the worst thing that could have happened to me. The lights lit, the noise sounded and the credits started to tick over – into the hundreds, into the thousands, into the tens of thousands. It wasn't the jackpot but it was pretty close: I'd won $54,000.

Seeing those credits on the machine felt strange. I didn't feel like I'd won – after all I hadn't – nor did I feel like I'd lost. As far as I was concerned I didn't need any cash, I just felt like I had at the end of any other drug-fucked day.

I guess one good take-away from this bender was at the end of the week we'd managed to smoke all of the crystal meth and I wasn't going to be a drug dealer. When we got to the end of the last bag, I actually felt relieved. Maybe subconsciously that's why we smoked it all.

Finally the party ended – or more correctly paused – when I had to go to Japan for the first fight of my new contract. I'd be facing Tsuyoshi Nakasako, a journeyman Japanese fighter, atop the card at a smaller annual event in Shizuoka, southwest of Tokyo.

When I went up against Nakasako I hadn't thrown a punch or raised much of a sweat (except maybe *the* sweats) since the K-1 victory, and I was heavier than I'd ever been before. I didn't have any real problems with Nakasako, though I did lean into one of his head kicks and it floored me. That flushed me with embarrassment. I got the finish in that fight near the end of the third round.

I'd taken Tokoa with me again, and after the fight we ended up talking about what life would be like if we didn't go home. The Japanese loved me – I was treated like a king as soon as I arrived at Narita Aiport. There was no

155

reason not to stay. I had no family I wanted to see, no job outside of throwing leather and more than enough money coming in. The idea was an exciting one, but it also made me feel oddly sad. It took me a little while to realise the thought of leaving Julie was making me melancholy. This realisation was unusual and uplifting, but also terrifying. I'd never been tied to anyone in my life before like this. My mates were my mates, but they'd come and go depending on the circumstances – there was no one else I thought about in the context of years, or maybe a whole lifetime.

When I returned to Sydney, I took Julie out for dinner and told her I wanted to buy a house with her, in Western Sydney. That was her home, and it would be my home. Who knows, maybe we'd even raise some kids in Sydney – some little Samoan–Scottish Australians one day.

It was around this time that Dixon asked me if he could borrow three hundred grand. He'd come across a great business opportunity and was selling a nightclub he owned in England to make it all possible, but the sale of the nightclub wasn't going through quickly enough to act so he needed a little bridging cash. It was to be a very short term loan, and I had faith in Dixon the businessman. He spoke like a siren, so off the money went, out the door.

Shortly after that, Dixon arranged another fight for me, this time in an event in Nagoya against Cro Cop. This was another fight I barely trained for, and one I got through because of my natural resilience to blunt trauma. Mirko was (and, at the time of writing, is still) famed for his head kicks, saying once in a press conference that his right leg was for putting you in the hospital, but his left leg was for putting you in the cemetery.

In that fight I ate what I reckon was one of the biggest left kicks the Croat ever dished out, and I ate it whole, ducking under a punch that never came, multiplying the force of my movement towards his leg by the velocity of his kick. It didn't put me in the cemetery but it did send me momentarily unconscious, with my hands raised as I fell.

I got up and continued the fight, but lost on points. The Japanese media went to town over Mirko's kick. I'd never been dropped in my K-1 career up to that point – I was a juggernaut, the immovable object, always moving forward. That was no longer the case.

When the journalists asked me what was wrong I told them he just got me – more power to Mirko. That was the end of the story. Only it wasn't the end of the story for me. I knew I was a better fighter than Mirko and I was deeply annoyed at being fat and unfit when I'd rolled into that fight against a quality opponent.

When I returned to Oz I started doing some fitness training but couldn't get back into striking sessions because

I'd aggravated an old hand injury from my street-fighting days. I'd sustained it when a guy I was busting fell into me and was biting chunks out of my stomach and chest. I started throwing punches into the top of this dude's head until I split my hand between the first and second knuckles, separating the skin and exposing the bone. My hand swelled up in the same place after the Mirko fight and soon it gave me too much grief to punch.

Shortly after I returned from Japan, Dixon called saying that K-1 wanted me to fight again in a couple of months. They were looking for the rubber match between Jérôme Le Banner and me to be the headline for an event they were mounting in the capital of his home nation, France.

I told Dixon I was injured, so they'd have to schedule something for me a little later in the year. Not long afterwards Dixon came to me again, saying Ishii-san really wanted me to take the fight. This was a key event for the company, in a new region, and they very much wanted to have the local hero face off against the man who'd knocked him out in the Grand Prix in which he'd been the heavy favourite to win.

I told Dixon it didn't really matter what they wanted, my ass wouldn't be ready until later in the year. I probably could've fought through the hand injury if I absolutely had to, but I'd just taken a fight against a real foe and

I'd rolled in fat and unready. I'd rather not do it against Jérôme frickin' Le Banner.

Two weeks before the Paris event, I was in New Zealand doing fitness training when I got a message from Hape saying he really wanted me to meet him at Dixon's new house. As I walked through my manager's place I imagined those cash flow problems he'd been having must have been over, and said as much.

'Yeah, things are okay,' he said.

'Can I get my money back then?'

'Not just yet. But there is something I have to talk to you about. They still want you to fight Le Banner.'

'When and where?'

'Same time, same place.'

Now, I don't know if he hadn't told the Japanese I wasn't fighting, or he hadn't been telling them with the necessary insistence, but either way I was pissed.

'I told you Dixon, I can't. I'm injured.'

'They wanted me to tell you that if you don't take this fight they'll be pretty upset.'

I didn't want the fight, so I started making demands. 'Okay, tell them this. I want to fly first class to Paris. Not business, but first. I also want two hundred and fifty grand for the fight.'

It was a number that just popped into my head. I thought I was highballing those guys, but knowing what I do now about K-1 fighters' pay, I was probably underselling myself.

'Mate, they won't go for it,' Dixon said in a small voice.

'Mate, then I'm not fucking fighting.'

'Is that it?'

'That's it.'

Dixon went away, presumably to call Ken Imai, and returned with a frown plastered across his face. 'Well, they're not going to give you the money. And not just that, if you don't take the fight your career may be over.'

You probably know me well enough by now to know that I don't respond to threats particularly well. After telling Dixon to relay the message that the entire K-1 organisation could go fuck itself, I was in my car and away. I was barely out of Dixon's driveway when he called and asked if I'd do it for a hundred grand.

'First class and two hundred and fifty. That's all there is,' I said, before hanging up.

I was barely out of Dixon's street when he called back again and said we had a deal. As I drove off it occurred to me that I'd just earned $190,000 specifically because I didn't listen to my bloody manager. I started thinking about the first contract I'd signed with the K-1, and wondered whether retaining Dixon as my manager really had been the best thing to do.

When I boarded my flight for Paris, who would I find next to me in first class but Dixon, who had somehow managed to negotiate himself a first-class seat too.

It turned out the flights were the best part of that trip. We were in Paris in the height of summer and the place was hot, smelly and the people didn't give a shit about me. In Japan I'd been loved by some and respected by all, but when I walked past Parisians, they just saw another thug.

The fight wasn't much fun, either. My hand didn't give me any issues but after receiving a light jab from Le Banner in the first round, my vision got all blurry. I went through that fight next to blind and even though I managed to drop Le Banner in the second round, he was picking me apart with long kicks and jabs that I was seeing only a microsecond before they thudded into me.

When I went into my corner after the second round, the fight doctor asked whether I could continue. I said I absolutely could. Even though I was almost blind, I had already dropped that big croissant once. I could do it again.

Dixon disagreed and threw in the towel. Now you might be wondering where a manager gets off making such decisions during a fight, and if you are, you'd probably understand a little bit of the volcanic rage that emanated from Hape as soon as the linen hit the canvas. Not to mention from me.

Soon Hape and Dixon turned their anger outward, at Le Banner's corner, accusing them of putting some sort of substance on their fighter's gloves that had blinded me. There was a short search for the Frenchman's gloves, which his corner said they'd thrown into the crowd. There was no finding them.

All I wanted was to get out of France. I was done with that fight, I was done with my team, and I was done with Le Banner.

I actually had no problem with Le Banner. If something had been put on his gloves, it was done to win a fight. I understood that. What I didn't understand was where I stood with Dixon and the K-1 organisation and even Hape – all the people who pushed for this fight I said I didn't want.

The flight home was the straw that broke the camel's back, and my faith in Dixon. We had dinner on the plane and at the end of the meal we were served some miniature fine cheeses, one of which looked like a red, oversized pill. It didn't look like the other cheeses so I left it for last, unsure of what to do with it.

When I saw Dixon pop that cheese into his mouth I followed suit, but I found it wasn't yielding as deliciously as the other cheeses had. It was tough, chewy and unpleasant.

As I watched Dixon pull the wax out of his teeth I realised my relationship with this guy was coming to an end. I was supposed to be the one who did the fighting and my manager was supposed to be the one who did everything else, which should have included knowing that you take the wax off before you eat the first-class cheese.

Chapter 10

AUCKLAND, NEW ZEALAND
2002

Mark was a huge favourite for the Japanese people. He never asked for the bright lights, and never talked himself up. He's the nicest man you can meet on the street, but if you hit him in the chin, you wake a demon. The Japanese loved that. They still do.

KONISHIKI YASOKICHI, FRIEND AND FIRST NON-JAPANESE SUMO TO REACH THE RANK OF *OZEKI*

I didn't go into my second K-1 Grand Prix with any intention of defending my title. I didn't intend not to, either; it was just that the four months after the Paris flight flew by and I wasn't counting the days leading up to the GP by training sessions, but by calls to Dixon asking for my money back.

Jules and I had decided it was time to move out of the apartment that Hape had arranged for us, and buy our own place. Back then I had no understanding of mortgages or brokers: I thought the only way to buy a place was the way I did it with my parents' house – hand over the cash amount whole, as you might buy a sandwich or a beer.

Dixon had stopped returning my calls after we got back from Paris and I was growing more and more annoyed, especially when news stories started emerging about how David Tua had been ripped off by his manager, and there was nothing Tua could do to get his money back.

One day I called Dixon's place and Ray answered. I told Ray to tell Dixon that he'd better get my fucking money together, and soon.

'You gave money to Dixon?' Ray laughed down the line. 'Was it money to pay back what Dixon owes me?'

I didn't know what the money had been for, but I was now convinced it wasn't for a slam-dunk business opportunity as he'd originally said. Maybe Dixon was paying back debts to Ray; maybe he was paying off gambling debts – which I'd heard he had a problem with – or maybe it was to pay for his new house. Whatever the reason, he owed me.

I didn't want to go around there – because if I did there was a serious possibility Dixon might end up with a fork in his eye, but I did want the debt settled right now. My anger over the situation simmered until one day, when I was having drinks with some mates who had previously been very useful in settling such situations, it bubbled over. I told these blokes about my predicament.

'We can put that motherfucker in a car boot for you if you like? If he has any money, he'll give it to you then, I promise that,' one of the guys said.

I seriously considered the offer. While it was seductive, it was an old-me solution. I didn't want to be involved with any more criminal shit; I wanted to be a civilian and deal with things the way civilians did. Besides, if Dixon was getting stuffed into the boot of a car, I hated to think someone else would get the pleasure of doing it.

A few days after that drink I walked into a legal practice in Campbelltown and told a lawyer about what had happened. A few weeks later Dixon's lawyers and mine were sitting across from one another, discussing terms.

I found out that mine was a long way from being the only debt Dixon had accrued and after a lot of to-ing and fro-ing with his lawyers, my people recommended taking a lesser sum, as the full $300,000 may not ever be recoverable. I asked for two hundred grand. Dixon baulked, but what sealed it was when I held up a newspaper with the story about David Tua and his manager on the cover.

'That could be you, Dixon,' I said to him. 'Do you want to be in the paper?'

My father and mother moved from Samoa to Auckland in 1965. This is one of the only family photos I have and if you've read the book you will understand why. When I was born in 1974 I had an older sister, Victoria (*far right*) and two older brothers, Steve (*bottom left*) and John (*bottom right*). That's me on my mother's lap. The photo looks serene but ours was a house of hunger and abuse. As I grew up, I didn't love school but I did like playing rugby league for the Mangere East Hawks 1989 under-sixteen team (*I am third row, second from left*). Any chance of making the Junior Kiwi team disappeared when they found out I'd been in prison.

I won my first K-1 Oceania title in Melbourne in 2000. Lucy Tui (*bottom left*), my first manager, was the most ecstatic at the result. Alex Tui (*bottom, second from right*) and Tokoa Mervin were also there. It was only a few years since I'd unknowingly turned professional (*top left*) and started mixing with fighters like Peter Graham (*top right*) and now I was heading off to fight in Japan. (Courtesy of Lucy Tui)

Sometime in 2001 the Japanese adopted me as one of their dudes. It all started after a fight with Ray Sefo, the undisputed king of the region, and the love affair hasn't ended yet. My 2001 K-1 Grand Prix win led to McDonald's commercials and presenting at the Japanese MTV Music Awards.

TOP: In 1999 I fought Chris Chrisopoulides. I may have lost the first five rounds but I kept getting back up and knocked Chris out in the sixth round. From back then to now, I never give up.

RIGHT: In UFC 135 in 2011 I went up against Ben Rothwell in Denver, USA. Rothwell was a fighter, an athlete and a talent, and I got over him through sheer bloody hard work.

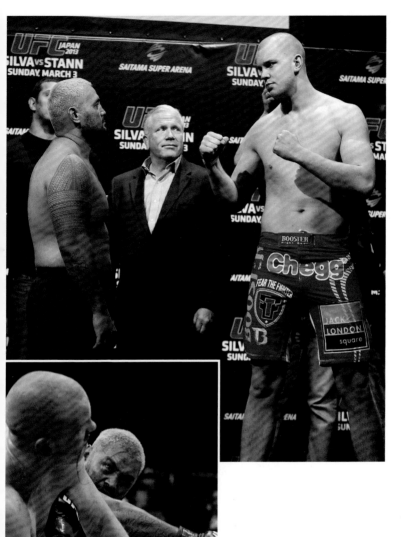

Dutch fighter Stefan Struve is a full foot taller than me. On 3 March 2013 in Saitama, Japan, I literally had to jump up with my left hooks to hit him in the face, but I did manage to land a few good ones. I won the fight and Stefan later tweeted an X-ray that showed a jaw so broken you could put your little finger through it.

RIGHT: After the Struve fight, the UFC asked if I'd fill in and fight Junior dos Santos, at the MGM Grand Garden Arena in Las Vegas. They only had to ask me once. I thought about the legendary battles that had taken place there – Tyson versus Holyfield, De La Hoya versus Mayweather, Pacquiao versus Hatton, now Mark Hunt against Junior dos Santos. The surrealism reached its peak when I met Tyson at the weigh-in and saw him in the crowd. BELOW: My fight in Brisbane on 7 December 2013 against Antônio 'Big Foot' Silva was epic. When I finished the third round I felt heat in both hands. I had three possibly broken limbs, a cut-up face – my blond hair had turned pink – and there was one more round to go. The fight ended in a majority draw but Dana White tweeted, 'Both Hunt and Silva win FON [Fight of the Night] and both get their win bonus and I might buy them both their own private ISLANDS!!!! Sickest HW fight ever!!!' I'm still waiting on that island.

TOP: Getting pumped before my fight against Roy Nelson in Japan on 20 September 2014. Roy was the one man in the UFC who made me look svelte.

BELOW: He's a big bloke, Fabrício Werdum, tall and experienced. I didn't have much time to prepare for UFC 180 in Mexico City on 15 November 2014. Some people were saying I wouldn't be able to hit him. I was too short, and Fab was too good. I was too old, too fat. I took the first round of that fight, but I got knocked out in the second. Clean. Well done, Fab, you got me good.

I love being a dad and I love being a husband. Home is where my life happens now. I never thought I'd find a place where I could be more comfortable than in a ring, standing across from a man with his fists raised, but I'm slowly making my way to other people's version of normal life. I look at these little smiling kids of mine and I look at my wife and I know I am living a good life.

We got an offer for a little more than $170,000 and, after a strong recommendation from my lawyers, I took the cash. When the time came to sign the agreement I looked at this slimy bastard who'd tried to take off with my cash and saw two things: a lack of remorse on his mug and an expensive-looking watch on his wrist.

'I'll take that too,' I said of the watch.

Dixon was shocked, but he handed it over. He knew I wasn't fucking around.

When Ben, the guy who's helping me put this book together, approached Dixon about the debt, Dixon said he had no recollection of this event. His version of events was that he borrowed the three hundred grand, and then paid it back – simple as that.

I messaged Dixon when I heard this, saying I was sorry he'd had the opportunity to tell his part of the story, but chose to keep repeating the same line. I really was sorry, too. I wasn't angry, but sad. I felt for the guy. He obviously got caught up in some shit he couldn't handle, and I'm not just talking about his debt to me.

I hope Ray Sefo will get to that point one day too, where he can simply pity Dixon. It might take a while, though. Those two were like family, until Ray found out a trust account he thought had between $200,000 and $400,000 in it was actually $7000 in arrears. Dixon was accessing the funds without Ray's knowledge although he claims he 'always paid the money back one way or the other'. Ray told Kiwi paper *Sunday News* that he – 'pray[s] for Dixon's soul every day, because he's going to end up in hell'.

By the time I headed to Japan to qualify for the defence of my K-1 Grand Prix title, I was without a manager and considerably less prepared than I'd been the year before. To be honest, though, I didn't really care that much about what happened. I'd already won the Grand Prix, I was already contracted and I was already a big name in Japan.

The previous year there had been a number of different ways a fighter could pick up a berth for the Grand Prix, but now there was just one – succeed in a single elimination tournament at the newly opened Saitama Super Arena. The sixteen best fighters would be invited, with half going into the main event a couple of months later.

I was drawn against Mike Bernardo, and even though my training had been almost non-existent I was pretty confident of getting over him. He fought pretty well in what ended up being a lethargic fight. I was the aggressor, but I didn't fight a particularly nuanced fight, basically just trying to butter him up with jabs and put some right-hand finishing bombs on him. I never managed to get one on him in the three regular rounds, and he got some good counter shots in.

While the judges made their deliberations I thought my campaign might be over before it had even begun, but they called a draw. In the extra round I did find that big swing, dropping him and taking the decision win. I almost felt like apologising to Mike when the announcer said my name.

Oh well, on we go.

In the press conference preceding the big event, the Japanese media wanted to know what kind of training I was doing for my defence.

'I'm mostly concentrating on sleep training,' I said.

There were follow-ups of course.

'Hunto-san, can you please tell me how you do this sleep training?'

'Yeah, basically what you do is you think about training really, really hard, and when you think you can't think about it anymore, then you go to sleep.'

The newspaper stories the next day talked about hyperbaric chambers and visualisation and the power of extreme concentration. I do love the Japanese.

I guess it was true that visualisation had helped me win the last Grand Prix, but when I walked into the Tokyo Dome for my second GP I wasn't thinking about Jérôme Le Banner's head and how it could be removed, I was thinking about what kind of meal I was going to have when the night was over. I'd found a good steak place close to where we were staying, and when I walked into the ring to fight my first opponent, Stefan Leko, the German–Croatian I'd beaten the year before, I was thinking about whether I was going to have mushroom or pepper sauce.

Stefan kicked the shit out of my legs in that fight. I was heavier than the year before and less mobile than I should have been when the fight began, but after battering my thighs, knees and calves with heavy kicks in the first round, I was moving around like a mummy. I still had my little power-dash, though. I know I don't look like I do, but I've always had a couple of those in me in a round. I'm plodding towards you and then all of a sudden I'm up on you like cholesterol.

I'm not sure what the scoring would have been in the first two rounds of that fight, but it became academic when, in the third round, I threw a little left hook that caught the German flush on the nose, sending him to the ground. He stumbled to neutral corner and tried to take the mandatory eight count, but mid-count found himself once again on the floor, with his scone lolling around like a bobble-head.

That was that. On we go.

Almost as soon as the fight finished the bruises came – blue, black and purple patches spreading up and down from my knee. As they grew the news came that my next opponent would be Jérôme Le Banner.

This frickin' guy!

A long, strong fighter with some of the most vicious leg kicks in the world, Jérôme could do some serious damage to my legs if he wanted to.

'Reckon he'll have a go at these?' I asked Hape, pointing to my bruises.

'Wouldn't you?' he asked.

Me? Nah, I'd probably still try for his chin.

My question was answered in the first second of the fight. When we got to the middle, I put my hand out so he could meet it with a glove touch, but not only did he leave me hanging, he threw a heavy right kick, straight to my knee.

Okay then you big French prick, let's do this.

I leapt and put a nice big opening flurry on him but he weathered it pretty well. We traded fairly evenly, until, late in the first round, he swung a right leg kick that I checked, but instead of feeling the slap of his shin against mine, I heard and felt a snap, as though an elastic band had broken in my knee.

When I put my foot back down my leg wobbled and I almost went to the canvas. From then I couldn't push off the leg. I knew something serious was up. So did Jérôme, who proceeded to batter that leg at every opportunity.

Each time I checked one of his kicks, a pulse of heat spread through my body. Something was really jacked up.

When I got back to my corner I told Hape what was going on, and he said I would probably have to get the KO if I was going to win. That was always Hape's strategy, but in this instance it seemed like prudent advice.

When I got back out there for the second round, I was street fighting. Every punch was thrown with a view to separating Le Banner's head from his neck, with wild intent. Some whooshing punches flew just past his nose, which brought gasps from the crowd, but not the decapitating effect I was looking for.

For the rest of the fight Le Banner did his thing, banging the shit out of my leg and tagging me with fast punches while I lumbered past him, then scooting away before I could retaliate. I grew more and more frustrated, until I ended up hip-throwing him on the ground in the clinch. He responded by getting up and throwing a heavy step-kick that landed flush on my injured knee. I crumpled to the ground.

I was fresh out of ideas. I was up against the ropes for much of the second round and, at one point, I walked into the corner and put my hands on the ropes to support myself. When Le Banner came at me, I braced myself on the ropes and threw a vaulting front kick.

Needless to say that didn't work.

Near the end of the fight I was about as mobile as a Romero zombie, and my only chance was to wait for the Frenchman to walk into my danger zone. Just after the strikes marking that there were ten seconds left in the fight, he did. I threw the combo I'd been looking for all fight – a left uppercut that landed in his armpit and a right hook that smashed right across his jaw. He fell to the floor, but he did manage to get himself up again as the final bell was tolling. With blood streaming from his nose and mouth, he raised his hands high. The Frenchman had taken the match, properly avenged his GP loss and had pretty much ended my K-1 career.

When Le Banner went into the final, his only loss over his last 22 fights had been against me the year before. Once again, however, it wouldn't be his year, losing in the final to Ernesto Hoost.

It had been an old-guard final, but there were two new fighters on the scene, who were knocked out in the early rounds, who would represent what K-1 would soon become. Those men were Bob Sapp – a 180-kilogram former NFL player who looks like a huge condom crammed full of walnuts, and Semmy Schilt – a seven-foot giant with destructively long and heavy limbs.

By 2002, K-1 was losing traction to Pride so its organisers

had started appealing to the Japanese appreciation of pageantry to stay relevant.

The relationship between Pride and K-1 was delicate and complicated. They were fiercely competitive organisations, but also often shared the same TV partner and were required to come together in huge co-productions, with the first such event being known as *K-1 Dynamite!* or *Pride Shockwave*, depending on whom you speak to.

Held a few months before the 2002 K-1 Grand Prix, *K-1 Dynamite!* was mounted on a scale that is still yet to be surpassed for a mixed martial arts event. Ninety-one thousand people crammed into the open-air Tokyo National Stadium for a night of spectacle (they even had an opening ceremony, with a torch relay that ended when Hélio Gracie, the great progenitor, re-lit the Olympic cauldron) and fights, some of which were held under K-1 rules, and others under Pride rules, which are very similar to the rules the UFC uses now.

When I saw those Pride fights I was intrigued. It was a whole new style of fighting: smaller gloves, fewer rules, no stopping because the fighters had ended up in a grapple or had fallen to the floor. It seemed much closer in style to the kind of fighting I'd experienced in South Auckland.

The other factor governing the relationship between Pride and K-1 was their dealings with the Japanese underworld, known as the *yakuza*. None of us *gaijin* knew exactly what was going on behind closed doors, but every so often we'd see a glimpse of the underlying structure of the two fighting organisations and, sometimes, as was the case when my K-1 contract came to an end, we even saw the full force of what the *yakuza* were willing to do to achieve their desired outcomes.

Before any of that, though, I had a snapped posterior cruciate ligament to deal with. When I limped backstage after the Le Banner fight, my knee began swelling up quite badly. The fight doctor sorted me out with some painkillers for the night, but that was pretty much it for treatment for a good few months.

I've never been one for complaining about injuries, and this was no different. My knee got more and more swollen as the days passed, but I assumed this was like any other little niggle you might pick up after fighting twice in a day. Turns out it wasn't, though.

Before the 2002 GP, Julie and I had made plans to go out and see a bit of the world after the tournament. When I won the GP in 2001, I also won a first-class trip to Japan for two, which we managed to exchange for multiple business-class flights. This enabled us to bring some friends to Japan for the GP, but it also meant the two of us could fly on to the US and Europe when the tournament was done.

In LA and London Jules and I ate and drank like Caesars, never looking at a price tag the whole trip. One night when the fire alarm in our London hotel kept going off, we just grabbed our bags and moved to the hotel next door, despite the fact that the rooms were £1300 a night. Fuck it – it was only money. It came easily, why should it not go in the same fashion? It was a trip I'll never forget. It ended up costing $150,000, but I don't regret a minute of it.

We went up to Scotland to meet Julie's cousins, and I'd never seen a country quite so enchanting. Jules and I hired a driver to take us out to Loch Ness, and while he told us about the region I whispered into her ear, saying, 'Close your eyes.'

Our guide kept talking and she started to stifle girlish giggles. The dude sounded exactly like Sean Connery's James Bond. It was as though James had a twin brother who'd missed naval recruitment and had ended up in hospitality.

When we got out onto the loch it felt like there was no one else in the world. The soft, rolling hills disappeared into haze, like a video game with a short draw distance, and when the sun appeared it came in soft panes, diffused by the clouds.

I was so happy there, with Julie, in that moment. We were happy. I'd had relationships before but they were highly combustible affairs. I'd never really known someone who could be at peace like that – not my mates, not my girlfriends, not anyone.

We could just sort of be there, together, and we'd be happy. We didn't need to be doing anything, we were just happy enjoying the loch. I wasn't sure life could get better than that.

Perhaps I should have asked Julie to marry me there and then – it would have been romantic, classic. It didn't occur to me, though. I know that some things occur to me later than most.

I ended up asking Julie some years later, at home over a box of chicken and without any forethought. I have no regrets, though. She's my wife now, and my proposal epitomised the way we enjoyed spending time together.

Another aspect of that overseas trip I enjoyed was the frigid northern European temperature. It felt like my knee had been getting hotter and hotter each day since the Le Banner fight, and I only really got relief from it when I stepped outside into the chilly air.

When we got home I was happy. I was happy in our little apartment, happy in Western Sydney, happy with Jules and happy to do some training. When I did get back to training, though, something had changed. I wasn't in shape, which was to be expected, but I couldn't get any traction from my left leg.

When Auckland Auimatagi floored me with a leg kick during a sparring session I knew something was really buggered. I went to the doctor and discovered I'd torn the posterior crucial ligament in my knee. I'd be on the shelf for a year.

With too much time on my hands and a healthy bank account by my standards, of course I hit the pokies hard again. First it was an outgoing trickle of cash, then a torrential gush. Tens of thousands flew away until, thankfully, one day Dave and I walked past an internet café that was offering LAN gaming. We walked in and it was like we were stepping into a secret society. All the dudes hunched over their computers were silent and still, except for infrequent quiet calls of disgust or glee and a crescendo of excitement for a few moments, then they resumed their silent poses.

The place looked like a crack house, with people passed out under tables, full ashtrays and empty bottles, and chip packets strewn around, but the players' dedication to their screens was enticing. Most of the Asian blokes (and they were pretty much all Asian blokes) were playing the same game, the multi-player first-person-shooter Counter-Strike.

Counter-Strike seemed exceedingly simple at first. The game was round-based, each round starting with the players choosing to be a terrorist or a counter terrorist, and fitting themselves out with some weapons before being dropped into a designated area – terrorists in one area, counter terrorists in another. The game finished when all the players on one side were dead, or when a team's objective had been fulfilled.

This game spoke to me. This game spoke to us. Dave and I jumped on a computer and we were there for hours. It seemed that with each round we played, the game revealed another level of depth. Every map had its own points of tactical importance; each weapon was useful in certain areas; and there were numerous tricks – fast-switching weapons, crouching behind walls, entering rooms after throwing flashbang grenades – that kept me a little longer in each round and with a slightly higher kill-to-death ratio.

There was a visceral aspect of the game that I liked, too. When you found yourself in a gunfight, things happened very, very quickly. The good players seemed to be able to get a crosshair on their opponent's head with preternatural speed. When I first started playing there were many times I'd fire on an opposing player who hadn't even seen me, and find myself dead. It felt like they were cheating. I know they weren't, though, because eventually I got to that crazy, twitchy level of speed.

I figured out that I liked to play CS the way I liked to fight, choosing to equip myself with the AWP (Arctic Warfare Police) – the big heavy sniper rifle – and the slow-firing but high-calibre Desert Eagle pistol as my weapons. My CS game was all about the one shot that would take you out.

For the first few weeks Dave and I played in that café, then we moved to late-night LAN parties, then we got our own gaming PCs. It was a good scratch, for that gambling itch, that Counter-Strike, almost as good as the pokies and a shitload cheaper, although perhaps it was even less sociable than the pokies. Woe to the person who talked to me during a round, and death to the person who talked smack to me when I'd just died.

There was one particularly embarrassing moment in my CS life when I was performing poorly in an online session and some keyboard warrior kept riding me and riding me. Things got heated and I ended up asking this dude where he lived. He told me, and to my delight his place was just round the corner from me.

When I got to this guy's house, a ten-year-old opened the door. I asked the kid where his dad was, and he said he was at work. I went home with a face so red it was about to spontaneously combust.

I loved CS, and it did keep me from drinking and gambling, but it seemed my life was always going to be a game of whack-a-mole. Any time I'd find a solution to a problem, some other bullshit was just around the corner.

Victoria was the one who called me. She said Dad was dying and he wouldn't go to the hospital. He'd been diagnosed with cancer, but was refusing any treatments and he was starting to rot, stinking up the house.

I didn't want to know about it.

'Dig a hole in the garden and chuck him in it. Wait till he's dead if you're feeling generous,' I told her.

I bought him that house. I'd done my son's duty. In my mind, that motherfucker lived in a locked box that existed only in the past, not the present.

'You have to come over and help,' Victoria pleaded.

I didn't understand why it fell to me. Even when I got to New Zealand and saw the silent, brooding husks of my brothers – in no shape to help anyone – I still resented that I was needed. I didn't want to engage with my family. I didn't want to know what was happening in John's or Steve's or Victoria's lives, and I certainly didn't want to have to think about the old man, or Mum, who was then incapacitated after a series of strokes.

If they were away from me physically, they would be away from me mentally. Ever since I was a child I'd been able to choose which thoughts would go so deeply into storage that they didn't even exist anymore. I had a capacity

– a gift as I see it – to put things aside and not think about them except when forced to. I knew being able to do that wasn't normal, nor would it help most people, but it kept me going.

I'm sure it helps me as a fighter. No matter what might have happened to me in the ring or what my record may be, I've always thought I was the world's greatest fighter. I can forget losses very easily.

I guess this gift came from my father. I don't really feel pain and fear either, and that's probably something he gave me too. In a hideous way, my father has probably been the most important figure in my fighting career.

When I got to the house, Dad absolutely stank. He smelled like death, and he was little more than a sack of saggy skin and brittle bones. I didn't say anything to him when I picked him up and tossed him over my shoulder. I didn't feel much either – he weighed nothing, and he meant nothing.

As I've already described, the devil took my father's soul, but the question of his body was left to me. There are costs associated with getting rid of a body and while I had money, I didn't want any more of it to go to that old rapist.

The Hunts stepped in – Dad's brother and cousins – saying that the old man had to be buried, not cremated, as some of us kids wanted. They also tried to absolve Charles Sale Hunt's sins, posthumously painting him as a kind and moral man.

Victoria was the one who finally said Dad should have a proper burial. The task of speaking at his funeral was also left to her. She said what she could, not what she should. I can't imagine what that job must have been like for her, but at the time I just felt relieved the task wasn't mine.

I didn't know many people at the funeral and the ones I did were mostly from his church. As I was leaving, an older Samoan woman approached me, claiming she was my sister.

I asked Victoria if this was true, and she said it was news to her, but most likely true. The stories flew around after Dad's death about repeated infidelity. It turns out this woman was one of at least three other siblings.

I wasn't warm to her. I didn't need any more siblings. I didn't need any more cousins or uncles either. I didn't even want the brothers and sisters I already had. I didn't want any more hands out, any business proposals, any reunions, any catching up, or anything to do with my old life. I just wanted to get home to Australia.

Chapter 11

TOKYO, JAPAN
2002

> After negotiations had gone to shit, Daisuke [Teraguchi, K-1 head of
> fighter relations] and two goons came to Auckland to meet with me.
> [Daisuke] said, 'You don't know what you're doing, Glenn. You must
> be careful. People go missing all the time in this business.' I stuck
> my finger out and said, 'If you want to do it, do it now then.' I was
> mixing up my *yakuza* lore; I was pretty pissed by then. I spent a lot
> of time looking over my shoulder the next time we went to Japan.
>
> **GLENN ELLIOTT, EX-MANAGER (SORT OF)**

The last fight of my K-1 contract was in Las Vegas; a place
that, for a poker machine addict like myself, was pretty much
heaven and hell rolled up in one 24-hour-a-day, neon-lit ball.

If you haven't been to Vegas, there are pokie machines
at the airport, there are pokie machines in the car rental

offices, there are pokie machines in the gas stations and the fast-food outlets, and there are certainly pokie machines in the Bellagio Hotel, where my suite was. If my fighting career primarily took place in Vegas (or if I really understood how to play *pachinko*) I'd now be in more debt than the US federal government.

I was in Las Vegas for a week and I spent . . . a lot. I don't know how much, but it was a fortune. I did so much gambling I never even got into the local time. It was just too easy to be out gambling and drinking all night and sleep in a darkened room during the day. I even missed my weigh-in for the fight because I was too busy gambling. The commission sat around for almost an entire day waiting for me to turn up, eventually catching me when I stumbled back to my room to sleep in the afternoon. They had to pretty much drag me down onto the scales.

The fight was against Gary 'Big Daddy' Goodridge, a heavy-hitting Canadian journeyman who would finish his kickboxing career with a record of 12–24–2 and, sadly, a diagnosis of dementia pugilistica.

I fought with heavy strapping on my left knee and was still moving pretty slowly, but that wasn't the reason I didn't take Gary out. He was the kind of guy who got stopped and I was the kind of guy who did that stopping, but I was coming back from injury. I'd only been able to train back home for a few weeks beforehand and when I got to Vegas I'd only managed a couple of light training sessions in my suite.

I beat Goodridge, but when I returned home after the fight I was out of sorts and low on motivation. I'd fucked around in that fight and wasn't sure I could get myself up for another K-1 tilt. I had money and I'd proved I could beat the best K-1 fighters. I didn't feel the need to keep doing it.

I also felt the K-1 was ripping me off. There were rumours flying around that managers were deliberately and habitually screwing fighters over, and I knew of some instances in which managers earned more than their fighters. The conventional wisdom was that the K-1 had fostered that disparity, too, trying to keep all the fighters lean and dependent on both a pay cheque and their managers.

I'd become a big name in Japan and had also won the biggest tournament of them all. I started feeling like I no longer wanted to fill up stadiums at sixty grand a pop. I didn't mind telling people I was done with K-1, either. I was ready to be plucked by the then surging Pride Fighting Championships.

I didn't have a manager for a while after Dixon, but lucrative martial arts organisations are like nature in that they abhor a vacuum. A Pride representative managed to track down a guy called Glenn Elliott, a Kiwi TV producer who'd been coming to some of my events with a view to making a documentary about me. When he fielded that call, I guess he became my manager of sorts.

For many years K-1 and Pride had worked in concert, both relatively happy with their piece of the pie, but in 2003 both organisations were in tumult. K-1 boss Ishii-san had been arrested for tax evasion, an issue that, supposedly, had been a by-product of an obsession to generate enough money to sign Mike Tyson to K-1. On the other side of the equation, Naoto Morishita, the long-time boss of Pride's parent company, Dream Stage Entertainment, had died in suspicious circumstances and many were speculating that the death might have been over how Pride should be run, and by whom.

Little did I know that Miro Mijatovic, another Australian in the Japanese fight game, was seeing close up how heavily involved the *yakuza* were in martial arts in Japan, and especially Pride during that time. A Sydney-born Australian with a Croatian background, Mijatovic had worked as a resource and infrastructure lawyer in Tokyo until he changed professional tack, starting a sports management company, with Aussie swimmer Ian Thorpe and my old foe Mirko 'Cro Cop' Filipović on his books.

After working with Cro Cop, Mijatovic saw there was a great amount of money to be made outside the K-1/Pride duopoly and brought in a number of disgruntled foreign MMA fighters to an annual Japanese MMA and pro wrestling show called Bom-Ba-Ye (named after a Lingala phrase that translates into 'kill him' which the Congolese people used to spur Muhammad Ali on against George Foreman in the Rumble in the Jungle in 1974), which was hosted by former pro wrestler and politician Antonio Inoki.

The show included a who's who of international fighters, including Lyoto Machida, Rich Franklin, Josh Barnett, Semmy Schilt and perhaps the most famous Pride fighter of all time, Fedor Emelianenko, who had previously been signed to Pride but could fight on the Bom-Ba-Ye card due to a contract technicality.

Normally the Bom-Ba-Ye cards would be accepted by the *yakuza* clans involved with K-1 and Pride, as long as the events didn't happen on their turf (most Bom-Ba-Ye events happened in Kobe), but this Mijatovic card involved too many of 'their' assets. Although the *yakuza* seem to prefer to operate subtly, the affront that Mijatovic had brought to them apparently warranted a similarly harsh response. After the event, Mijatovic was held at gunpoint in his hotel for three days, until he signed all of his foreign fighters over to Pride in iron-clad exclusive deals.

At the same time Pride was also trying to woo me, but I was getting more carrot than stick. A female executive at Pride named Yukino reached out to Glenn with an offer for me – a quarter of a million dollars per fight. This was a new sport and it was more money, so there wasn't any part of me that didn't like the offer.

Glenn voiced concern as to whether I could move to this sport, which involved ground fighting, submissions and wrestling. As he pointed out, I'd be thirty by the time I'd have my first MMA fight, and I had no history of martial arts training in anything other than kickboxing.

'Do you think you'll be able to adjust to it?' he asked.

I thought I'd be fine. With far fewer rules than in K-1, these Pride fights looked a lot more like the street fights I'd had in South Auckland. At the time, I'd never even really heard of Brazilian *Jiu-Jitsu*, *vale tudo* or catch wrestling and perhaps I'd underestimated how different Pride would be from K-1, but I just said to Glenn that I'd be sweet.

Go set it up, mate.

The structure of my K-1 contract dictated, however, that they would have an opportunity to match any other offer I might receive, and when Glenn told Ishii-san about the Pride offer, he invited us all to travel to Japan to explain what they could offer. When we arrived, Glenn and I had to suffer interminable meetings in which we were offered the stars, including a potential fight against Mike Tyson, if I would only re-sign with K-1. I told Glenn I was ready for a new challenge so they'd have to back up a Brinks truck to keep me in kickboxing, but no matter how much they said I was an important asset to them, they'd still only shift to twenty or thirty grand more per fight. This wasn't nearly enough.

The trip to Japan coincided with an event K-1 was hosting at the Saitama Super Arena, and I was invited as a guest. When I got there I found myself seated next to Shannon Briggs, then IBU world heavyweight boxing champion.

'You see Mark, you sign with us and you can fight Shannon Briggs. First Briggs, then Tyson,' Ken Imai told me that night.

Fighting Briggs would be great, fighting Tyson would be a dream, but that was only going to happen if they could beat the Pride offer of a quarter of a million a fight. It was something they wouldn't budge on.

'No Mark, you are ours,' Ishii-san would say to me. I certainly didn't see it that way.

On the last night of the trip I was wholly frustrated with dealing with a group of businessmen who saw me as property. Glenn suggested that he, Tokoa, Dave and I head out and get some drinks into us. It sounded like a great idea to me.

We found a small underground restaurant in Roppongi where we thought we could hide from any prying eyes and get well and truly stuck into the piss. We knocked back sake, beer, whiskey and highballs in what we thought was anonymity, but even though there were only a few tables at this place, a couple across from us recognised me and wanted to sit with us.

Three sheets to the wind, we begrudgingly accommodated them. Conversation would have been problematic even if they had perfect English, what with all of us slurring our speech and mostly speaking nonsense, but with them having almost no English (and us even less Japanese) we were reduced to hand gestures and monosyllabic words.

Well past midnight, the lady at our table started trying to say something to me. She really had something to get off her chest and even though I couldn't understand her, she was going to get her piece out. When she finished, neither Glenn, Tokoa, Dave nor I had any understanding of what she'd said, but the man she was with apparently did, jumping up furiously and trying to throw his sake at her.

It didn't land on her, it landed on Tokoa, with the glass also escaping his hand and smashing on the ground. It took about three seconds for the small restaurant to descend into a scene of madness.

Tokoa was battling with the man who'd thrown sake in his face; the chef, who had come out to voice his displeasure over the broken glass, was being ridden like a horse by the man's wife; Dave was trying to usher me out onto the street; and Glenn was hiding in the toilets.

When the police arrived, the Japanese man who'd thrown the sake had given up on Tokoa and was attacking a cylindrical marble fountain at the entrance of the restaurant, trying to kick it over. Tokoa apparently wasn't done with him, though, so it was those two who were nabbed and frog-marched out of the restaurant by the cops.

As we walked up the stairs, I whispered to Tokoa, 'On the count of three, we'll all scarper up the street.'

There was a slight nod.

'Okay . . . one . . . two . . .'

Tooks was off, cutting a very wonky line through the Roppongi night, wheezing like the asthmatic he is, with the police in pursuit. It looked like he was going to make it, too, until he ran straight into a light pole.

DOOOOONNNNNNNG

'You boys go back to the hotel. I'll sort this out,' Dave said, hailing us a cab.

As we drove back to the hotel, I couldn't stop laughing, and I felt energised. All this negotiation and Japanese double-talk was exhausting, and I actually felt more comfortable where there were fewer rules, rather than more.

I would try out Pride and MMA. I was ready for something new.

When I arrived at the hotel, I got a call from Tokoa asking me to come and pick him up from the police station, as they didn't believe he was in Japan with me. When we got there, two funny things happened. The first was that we found the woman we'd been drinking with running out of the police station with a sheaf of papers, being hotly pursued by a group of cops like a scene from *Benny Hill*. The second was that Tokoa was released with no charge after I posed for photos with a seemingly endless line of cops.

When we returned home from Japan Glenn was served with a Japanese lawsuit for $750,000 by K-1's parent company. Even though it seemed the suit had no basis, we'd feared it might have been coming. It wasn't unusual for such a suit to be issued by a fighting organisation to a truant fighter, as they knew it could lead to an injunction to stop the fighter from fighting (and earning) until the suit was resolved.

It was a standover tactic, a threat. I don't respond well to threats. I told Glenn to tell the K-1 to go fuck themselves, and I told him to use those exact words. I'm not sure if he did, but either way, some K-1 representatives turned up in Auckland wishing to speak to him. Glenn took them to Tanuki's Cave, a Japanese restaurant and sake bar on Queen Street. They tried to get him into their confidence, explaining that he didn't understand how it all worked, and that things could be very good for him if he arranged for me to sign a new K-1 contract.

I'd never signed any contract with Glenn and therefore he wasn't really my manager, and even if he was, he certainly wasn't in a position to give away a couple of hundred grand a fight. He told them that without a huge bump-up in pay there was no way to proceed. That's when they threatened to bump him off. It was no idle threat, either, but Glenn told them it would probably be easier and safer to survive in Japan with the *yakuza* trying to kill you than it was to try to get me to change my mind when it had been well and truly made up.

A couple of months later Pride invited me to go to Japan to meet people from their organisation and officially sign my contract. When I arrived, they treated me the way I wanted to be treated. The new boss of Pride, Nobuyuki Sakakibara, invited me to dine with him and his lieutenants at a private dining room in some super-fancy hotel in Tokyo. When I arrived in sandals and shorts, the suited

Sakakibara-san didn't even bat an eyelid, welcoming me warmly and telling me I was now part of his family.

Well, now that we're family . . .

'Are you Japanese mafia or something?' I asked Sakakibara-san.

There was no answer, but there was a lot of uncomfortable ass-puckering and blank stares. When the conversation finally resumed, Sakakibara-san was at pains to explain that a meeting had taken place between himself and the K-1, and that the lawsuit had been resolved. I was now free to sign without any impediment.

When Glenn said he'd sought legal advice and he was pretty confident he could take this lawsuit on in court and maybe even counter-sue, Sakakibara-san went white.

'No, no, you must not! This has been resolved. This whole matter has been resolved,' he said.

That was that. I was a Pride fighter. After signing a four-fight contract, they gave me forty grand to go to California to train with legendary Dutch MMA fighter, former UFC champion and Pride colour commentator Bas Rutten, so I could learn how to fight on the ground. But I couldn't be bothered to go to California, so I pocketed the money and set out to find someone in New Zealand or Australia who could teach me all this MMA stuff Pride wanted me to know about.

When I got back to Sydney from Japan, a guy I used to play league with named Brendon, who knew I was about to fight in Pride, said I should check out a Brazilian *Jiu-Jitsu* (BJJ) competition in Manly. At that tournament I saw a couple of Kiwi kids I knew, Jamie and Tama Te Huna, beasting at this new type of fighting. It was there that I also met BJJ professor Marcelo Rezende, a Brazilian everyone seemed to know and respect, and one of his top black-belt students, Steve Oliver, who to this day is my trainer, and has been one of the most important figures in my fighting career.

I actually thought this kind of fighting was a pile of rubbish – a few good punches and these guys wouldn't be wriggling around quite so much anymore, grabbing feet and necks and whatnot. I didn't really respect them.

I was heading back to Auckland for a bit so Brendon suggested I visit Steve Oliver, who ran a martial arts facility there. I weighed more than 140 kilograms at the time, and when I met up with Steve he gave me a good look up and down. Sensing my disdain, he suggested we have a little bit of a throwdown. I had no problem with that idea. Steve weighed just over 90 kilograms and I was confident I could easily handle anything this bloke could throw at me.

I was wrong.

We had a good, hard grind and more than once Steve ended up on top of me, with me unable to do anything about it. When he was on me, he showed me a number of ways a man on top can hurt a man on the bottom – with fists, with feet and with knees, the latter he managed to grind into my face and neck a number of times in that first session.

When I walked away I had a much greater understanding of why so few kickboxers or boxers had ever made a successful transition into MMA. I had my work cut out for me.

Steve was a very good fighter, but he wasn't Pride good. He was a guy with a gym in the suburbs of Auckland. If he could grind me down, what kind of beating could Fedor give me? As was often the case, I thought about all this intellectually, but not viscerally. I was the best fighter in the world and it didn't matter what the rules were. I felt confident that I'd figure it all out once I was in the ring. This mantra was stamped across my mind like a brand.

In the lead-up to my first Pride fight, Steve and I flew to Sydney to train with Steve's professor, Marcelo. It was a hard, draining, confusing grind. I had an instinct for ground fighting, as I'd had a lot of experience with the street version in Auckland – but while my instincts were sometimes right, they were more often wrong. As Marcelo kept pointing out, the men I'd be fighting in Pride would be the best ground fighters in the world, not big South Auckland thugs. I needed to learn, I needed discipline and I didn't know what I was getting myself into, Marcelo would say.

Yeah, yeah, yeah.

The more I trained with Steve and Marcelo, the more Hape disliked them. Hape saw me as his guy, and he didn't want to share. He either couldn't or wouldn't understand that if I was going to succeed in Pride, I needed a lot of ground-fighting help.

Over the previous year I'd been feeling increasingly annoyed by Hape's attitude. He'd been bringing other Australasian fighters to K-1 events with a view to developing a little team, and while I was all for developing the Aussie and Kiwi fight scene, I'd have preferred it not to be while I was paying him. All the little issues started to pile up – per diems, fan gifts that never made it past Hape's hands, and the final nail in the coffin, finding out that Hape had been planning on training Olympic gold medal judoka and Pride fighter Hidehiko Yoshida in his stand-up fighting. Yoshida was to be my first opponent in Pride.

'Mark, it's just business,' Hape said.

It's just a conflict of interest, mate.

At the end of 2002 Pride invited me over to Japan to one of their biggest events of the year, Pride Final Conflict, where they were going to announce my signing. I checked in to the hotel as 'Mr X' (to keep the integrity of their surprise) and when I was finally brought into the ring and introduced, I saw my fighting future ahead of me.

The Pride-contracted heavyweights were introduced one by one after me, many of whom I would end up facing. When they introduced Russian fighter Fedor Emelianenko, the crowd roared and I could hear Cro Cop, who was standing next to me, muttering to himself. I didn't know exactly what he was saying – he was probably speaking in Croatian – but I got the gist.

This fucking guy.

Fedor was obviously the boss, the top of the pile, and Mirko wanted to knock him off it. I instantly wanted the same thing.

At that tournament I also encountered for the first time two American businessmen with whom I'd have my own, very different battles. Their names were Lorenzo Fertitta and Dana White, the two executives who now ran the Ultimate Fighting Championship, and they were in attendance because they'd lent one of their top fighters, Chuck Liddell, to Pride so he could compete against Pride favourite Quinton 'Rampage' Jackson.

Fittingly at the time, Liddell was stopped in the second round. It was an eye-opening experience, that night. Those Pride fighters were a completely different breed from the K-1 guys. They just seemed more intense. The fighting also looked very different. I probably understood what was going on in those fights less than most of the people in the crowd did, what with all the technical BJJ and wrestling. Passing guard, full mount, sprawls, arm bars, rear-naked chokes – none of it really meant anything to me yet.

A few months later I returned for my first Pride fight, which was to be part of an event called Critical Countdown at the 50,000-seat Saitama Super Arena. I would end up fighting more than half of my MMA fights at this arena.

In the press conference preceding the fight I was asked how much time I'd had fighting on the ground, and I replied honestly.

'About eight hours.'

There was a ripple of laughter through the crowd, and also from my fellow fighters up on stage. The one who was really giving out a good old belly laugh was Fedor.

'It was a good eight hours though,' I said. That was the moment I realised eight hours probably wasn't enough.

When Steve, Marcelo and I walked into the Super Arena, I didn't feel trepidation, I felt the same curiosity I'd felt when I had my first kickboxing fight back at DTMs, and also when that judge told me I was going away for my first stretch in prison.

'I wonder,' I thought as I walked through the crowd. 'I wonder.' I honestly didn't know what to expect.

An Olympic hero, a two-time gold medallist and a guy who was strongest where I was weakest, Yoshida was one of the biggest draws in Pride at that time, and when he came out in his judo *gi* the crowd gave huge cheers. They weren't silent when I came out in my kickboxing shorts either. Pride didn't give out charity money.

I was supposed to get a beating that night; it was supposed to be a baptism of fire. That's how the Japanese liked to do it. That's how they liked to bring people into the organisation.

After the referee's instructions we tried to touch gloves, but doing it with these MMA gloves for the first time, I botched it up and we sort of ended up holding hands. I really was as green as a lime spider.

When Goldy and Rogan call UFC fights these days, they sometimes call them 'striker versus grappler' contests, usually meaning that the fighters have a preference, rather than a complete disability. Nowadays it's almost impossible for someone to get into the UFC, let alone the upper echelons, with an almost complete lack of ground-fighting experience.

It wasn't like that then. I was going into this fight with less ground-fighting experience than most white belts, and Yoshida had more than 1000 judo matches as well as five Pride fights under his black belt.

I wonder. I wonder.

When the bell sounded we danced around for twenty seconds before Yoshida ran in for a single leg takedown. As I went to the ground, I managed to spin the Japanese fighter onto his back. I ended up in Yoshida's guard, which would be a preferable position for most fighters, but I had no idea where to go from there. Steve and Marcelo were yelling at me, but when I looked over at them in my corner, I couldn't understand a thing they were saying.

Yoshida locked in one of my arms and it looked like he was going to get me in an arm bar, but I managed, with pure instinct, to get my knee on his face and out of that position. There was more yelling from my corner, but it was like having Ikea instructions read to you in the original Swedish. As it turns out, it's pretty much impossible to undertake high-level Brazilian *Jiu-Jitsu* remotely.

Eventually Yoshida turned me into a weird body pretzel where I was on top of him, but with an arm and a leg wrapped up by his limbs. Eventually we worked our way into the corner and the ref decided to stand us up. We wheeled around for a little, and Yoshida went for the single again, but I saw it coming, bracing his shoulders and sending a big old knee at his big old head. I mis-timed the strike a little though, hitting him in the left collarbone, which snapped in half.

Kudos to Yoshida – he gave me no indication he had a broken bone and shot in again at my legs. Once more I stuffed the takedown, jumping into his guard. I could hear the yells of 'noooo' from my corner that time, but I was fighting my way now. If I was going to beat this guy it needed to be by way of fist to the face. I did manage to drop some big shots into the jaw of the former Olympic champion before he threw a triangle over me and eventually rolled me over for an arm bar.

He was a tough bastard, this Yoshida guy. He'd copped a broken bone, and still managed to beat me. This Pride thing was going to be no joke.

Five and a half minutes and it was all over. Earning fifty grand a minute didn't suck, but I thought the brass would be pissed at me and the other fighters would mock me. That wasn't the case. Both the executives and the fighters had encouraging words for me. There had been other guys from K-1 who had lasted seconds, not minutes, when they first got to Pride. I'd lost, but they reckoned I could give these blokes in Pride a run for their money.

I had four months until my next fight, and I spent a lot of that time practising takedown defence and escapes, which are basically moves designed for getting off the ground if you end up down there. Sounds easy, but that's not the case when you're in the ring with someone who's spent their entire life stopping you from doing just that.

My second Pride fight was against Dan Bobish, a giant American collegiate wrestler-cum–mixed martial artist with experience in a number of fighting organisations including the UFC. At 160 kilograms, Bobish was going to be the biggest bloke I'd ever fought and I had no doubt he'd try to get me on the ground.

He tried for the first minute or so of the fight to take me down, but I managed not only to keep him off me, but belt him with some pretty nice uppercuts and knees as well. I opened him up above the left eye with one of those and the ref stopped the fight, but only for a moment as the doctors deemed he was able to continue.

After the break Bobish did take me down, and there he lay on me for six or so minutes. Every so often he'd posture himself up so he could throw punches or knees at me. At one point I ended up in the turtle position, on my hands and knees, where he could throw knees at my head at his leisure.

I was so green, I had no idea how to get out of that position. Bobish kneed my head so many times I lost count, only stopping because – as he said after the fight – he was worried he might break his kneecap.

As Bobish moved up and down me, looking for more places to hit me, I kept trying to go through my mental files to match an escape to the position I was in. By the time I found something I thought would work, Bobish had moved again.

When I finally matched position and escape, Bobish, a guy who made me look like a league halfback, had exhausted himself belting me. We got to our feet, his hands and knees hurting from battering me and his gas tank well and truly exhausted. I was pretty gassed too, but I figured I only needed enough in the tank for a couple of punches, if I threw them correctly.

As Bobish lurched towards me, looking for another takedown, I popped him with a nice, sharp little uppercut. That rocked him. One knee to the head and one liver kick later and he was tumbling towards the ropes like a felled tree. He was done. There was no need to jump on him and inflict any further damage.

That was my kind of fight. He'd come at me and come at me with what at the time felt like endless undefended strikes to my head, but I stuck around. If I stick around long enough, I'll get you.

At the end of the fight Bobish was sent off to hospital, not because of the glancing uppercut or body kick that stopped him, but because he thought he'd blown his knee out.

When I got backstage I was greeted with cheers from the Brazilian ground-fighting contingent who, in their broken English, praised my escape and finish. When I joined Pride the other fighters welcomed me, but I knew they sniggered at me behind my back. They thought I was going to be an easy win for them like most of the kickboxers who came over to MMA, but that's one of the things I love about martial artists, they always give credit when credit is due.

'Escape, huh? Is good. Is very good,' Antônio 'Minotauro' Nogueira, one of MMA's most talented Brazilian fighters, said with a respectful handshake and bow when the fight finished.

It felt so good. Dan Bobish was a journeyman (and was cut from Pride after our fight), but he was a mixed martial artist and a ground fighter and I'd beaten him. I felt like I was now part of the club.

It would only take one more fight until I felt like I owned the club. My next bout was against one of the most famous MMA and Pride fighters in history – a guy who was on an eighteen-fight unbeaten streak against legendary fighters such as Quinton 'Rampage' Jackson, Kazushi Sakuraba, Dan Henderson and Mirko 'Cro Cop'.

I was about to take out the Axe Murderer.

Chapter 12

TOKYO, JAPAN
2006

Part of the reason Mark was so good at Pride was because he was always, always going forward. Always. It would freak out some of the other fighters, and that also meant they could never set their back foot against him, because if they ever did, Mark would be right up in their face. Not where you want to be.

BAS RUTTEN, UFC HALL OF FAME INDUCTEE AND PRIDE COMMENTATOR

I love living in Western Sydney. That place is heaven to me. There's no bullshit there. Everything you need is there, and nothing you don't. There are no Ferraris driving down Campbelltown's main street and no one looks twice when blokes like my mates and I walk down to the coffee shop. I don't get hassled by someone trying to get me in on their dodgy business or a cousin asking for a loan because they've been charged with sexual assault of a minor and they need to lawyer up. There is none of that shit.

I'd come to Western Sydney randomly, because of Hape and Julie, but I stayed because it made sense to me. I became increasingly convinced that I wasn't leaving Pride and their pay cheques any time soon, so here in Western Sydney, with love and calm in my life for the first time, Julie and I decided to start a family.

When I got back from my fight with Dan Bobish in November, I was planning on taking a few weeks out from training. I'd picked up an ankle injury in my first Pride fight when Yoshida got me in a toehold and I was going to try to rest it a little.

I was going to buy a house. I was going to start a family. The idea had come and gone, but now it was back. This was the right place and the right time. Jules and I were going to spend the holidays together. We ended up doing Christmas, but not New Year's.

I got the call on 28 December, with Yukino asking me if I could fill in on Pride's New Year's Eve event, which was usually the biggest of the year. Of course I could fight – I could always fight – but from my experience with the Mirko fight, this felt like opportunity calling.

'I am technically cleared, but I have this ankle injury which I'd like to get right, and I just fought Bobish, so . . .'

Of course she knew the game I was playing.

'What's it going to take, Mark?'

I asked for four hundred and fifty grand and six business -class flights to Tokyo. This could be a bit of a godsend – not only could I cash myself up, I could take the boys to Tokyo for a massive New Year's knees-up.

'That's it?'

'Yep.'

'Don't you want to know who you'll be fighting?' she asked.

Not particularly. I've never been concerned with who I'm going to be fighting, because I've never met a man I didn't think I could beat down. Besides, I couldn't train for a guy in three days, so his name was immaterial to me.

If they got the money right, then they could have me.

'You'll be fighting Wanderlei Silva.'

'Okay,' I said.

'Okay?'

'Okay.'

'Okay, well then, it's a deal.'

The boys and I were booked onto the next flight to Japan. I didn't really know much about Wanderlei Silva when I got that call, except that he was Brazilian, he was one of Pride's most popular guys, and he called himself the Axe Murderer. In his nineteen Pride fights Wanderlei was undefeated. I know now that I was probably put up against him just as a big body that could stay upright while it copped a beating, but when I left Sydney I was pretty confident of a win.

Wanderlei was a black belt in BJJ and judo, but he specialised in *Muay Thai* and liked to fight on his feet. Even though we were fighting a catchweight bout, Wanderlei was a natural light heavyweight, so I'd outweigh him as much as Bobish had outweighed me. That would help. Also, Wanderlei liked to stand toe-to-toe and throw down. He'd won twelve of his last thirteen fights by way of knockout, and, as the new boy to Pride, he might not know me well enough to know it's all but impossible to finish me.

It seemed impossible, but there was more pageantry at that Pride event than even the K-1 Grand Prix. The night kicked off with a single figure approaching a giant *taiko* drum, before ripping off his costume to reveal what looked like a nappy with a g-string. As he played the drum he was joined by a flock of other drummers, all wailing away perfectly in rhythm before building up to a crescendo, then the wall behind them disappeared to reveal the fighters on a giant, multi-level stage. The fighters were introduced one by one, and it was a murderers' row of talent: me, Dan Henderson, Kevin Randleman, Anderson Silva, Jens Pulver, Takanori Gomi, Mirko, Fedor, Nogueira and Wanderlei, who got the biggest cheers from the 50,000-strong crowd. The ceremony ended with fireworks. It was time for me to go to work.

I dropped Wanderlei early in the first round and managed to get a really solid escape on him after he took me down and tried to lock me in an arm bar. I was feeling pretty happy with myself after that one. When I extricated myself from him, Wanderlei lay on the ground waiting for me to come back to him.

I knew Silva loved an upkick, so I had to be wary of that, but I also really felt like jumping on that prick and wailing on him. I launched myself at him with an improvised attack that I think is unlikely to have been attempted in professional MMA before or since. I jumped up and tried to land my ass on Silva's head, as though I was at the swimming pool and the Brazilian was the water.

Randy Couture, who was doing the English commentary, called it the 'Atomic Butt Drop'. The crowd loved it, but it had little effect and I landed on my back. The round ended with me dropping him again, but I'd taken a decent amount of ground-and-pound damage from my back.

I dropped Wanderlei again at the beginning of the second with an uppercut and jumped on him as he fell, but he showed a solid chin and even managed to get on top of me again. I was exhausted when we started the last round, and accordingly we spent a decent part of the round with Wanderlei on top of me, even though he didn't really manage any significant damage.

Silva had certainly outwrestled me, but I thought I might have done enough with my hands to get the win. The Brazilian was a local favourite, though, and a veteran – so who knew how the judging was going to go.

Two of the three judges saw it my way. I'd arrived, man. I'd beaten one of the biggest names in the organisation and I tell you, Roppongi got the true South Auckland treatment that night.

When I returned home, Jules and I stuck our banner in the ground. We were getting a house and after that we were going to try for a kid. That was a pretty huge decision for me, but it just seemed right. Julie wanted to settle her life and I wanted what she wanted. I wanted it too, don't get me wrong, but without Julie I may have never found my way there.

When the mortgage brokers saw what I was earning in Pride they were happy to lend us a pile of cash, and I got exactly what I wanted – a mansion. Julie said we didn't need a house that big. She was right, too, and I knew it, but I wanted that place. I wanted lawns that needed a ride-on mower. I wanted multiple bathrooms. I wanted extra rooms that would just end up storing boys' toys. I wanted a 'Cribs' crib, man.

I found a guy to build a completely specced-out computer for me and set up a dedicated gaming room. That year I managed to put 40 Screaming Eagles on my Counter-Strike account, an honour that's only possible with more than 60 hours of play a week.

When Pride contacted me about my next fight they had the audacity to ask me to take a pay cut – from US$250,000 a fight to US$200,000. I'd just been paid more than double that and I'd knocked off one of their top guys after three days' notice, not to mention that I'd broken my finger in the process. The way I saw it, I did them a favour by fighting Wanderlei and my stock had been rising since I'd beaten him. If anything my price should be going up.

Pride continued with preparations for the fight, even though I told them I wouldn't be fighting on the cheap. To their credit, they did find perhaps the most enticing opponent possible for me – Cro Cop. I'd never forgiven Mirko for making me feel embarrassed at the K-1 event in Melbourne and I was desperately keen to avenge my 2002 Nagoya loss to him, but business was business and as I said to them again and again, my days of fighting on the cheap were over.

Despite this, the promotional wheels went into action. Billboards were erected, advertisements aired and articles were published, but at no point did I tell Pride I would be on that card for $200,000. The days, weeks and months went by, until it was December and I got a call from Yukino about flights.

'Flights come after money,' I told her, and hung up.

Yukino called back and said I could have my $250,000, but I told her we were well past that. Although a quarter of a million US dollars a fight was good money, I was angry about the attitude of ownership the Japanese fighting organisations had over their fighters.

There was so much money being generated – nearly 50,000 tickets had already been sold for the New Year's Eve fights and the television audience would probably be around 20 million, so why shouldn't a decent amount of it go to the fighters?

There'd always been rumours that the television companies gave the organisers a certain sum per fighter, and whatever amount the organisers could get the fighter to agree to below that, they could keep. I wanted to see how much financial wriggle room they actually had.

After that I got a call from another Pride representative, this time a lawyer.

'Hunto-san, how can we make this right?'

'I just want respect from you guys. I've been doing what you need me to do in the ring, now you need to do what you should out of it.'

'Okay, how do we do that? Do we need to come down there and see you?'

'That couldn't hurt.'

Three days later I was in the lobby restaurant of the Shangri-La Hotel in Sydney facing an interpreter, a couple of Japanese flunkies and the head of Pride FC himself, Nobuyuki Sakakibara. With me was a friend named Ben who'd been staying at my place. He'd lived in Japan as a Mormon missionary and had picked up a lot of the language.

The Pride people were dressed for business; Ben and I were dressed for Counter-Strike, which was on the agenda after we finished this meeting. While we negotiated there was a lot of private conversation on the Japanese side of the table, with the obvious assumption that a couple of coconuts like me and Ben wouldn't be able to understand their tongue.

Eventually Sakakibara-san said to me, via the interpreter, that $250,000 was the absolute limit of what they could offer and there was no point asking for anything more. I leaned over to Ben and asked if that was true. He said it wasn't.

'There's a lot going on on that side, and I didn't pick it all up, but they're trying to lowball you, man,' Ben said. 'There is more money; they've said that. I don't how much there is, but they think that because you've been on the shelf for a year and you don't have a manager, you'll go for the $250,000.'

I was sick of this shit. A quarter of a million was good money and I'd happily take it again after this fight, but they'd tried to stiff me – and right in front of me, no less. The old anger rose up, so I stood and pointed at Sakakibara-san.

'You're full of shit, man. You can shove this fight up your fucking ass,' I said to him.

Sakakibara-san spoke English, even though he sometimes chose not to, and started speaking – growling really – in Japanese in a way he hadn't spoken to me before. He didn't raise his voice, but he spoke with menace. When he was finished, it was my turn.

'This is my city,' I told Sakakibara-san sternly. 'Ben, tell these motherfuckers I'm going chuck them all in the harbour. And you,' I said, pointing at Sakakibara-san, 'are going in first. You can open a window, or go through the glass. Up to you.'

Ben spoke for the first time in, what I'm told was, really good Japanese. There were some red faces and a long period of silence broken only by piped music and the clinks of cutlery on fine crockery.

Eventually it was the interpreter who spoke.

'Mark, we came to make this right. How can we make this right?'

This was where a manager would have earned his keep, as I hadn't really thought that far ahead.

'Six hundred and fifty grand.'

The number just tumbled out of my mouth.

'And I want three hundred and fifty before you guys leave Sydney, too.'

I'd always had to chase K-1 for my money, and even though I never had such problems with Pride I thought it was better to be safe than sorry.

'And that's it?' the interpreter asked.

That was that. I asked them to please excuse us, as we had a very important meeting with some counter terrorists.

While Ben and I were playing Counter-Strike that afternoon I was wondering how the Japanese were going to respond. A few days later I found out, when more than half a million Aussie bucks landed in my account.

Apart from my K-1 GP match against Le Banner, I'm not sure I'd ever wanted to win a match more than in that fight against Cro Cop. I didn't really have any deep personal animosity towards the guy, but I couldn't get over the fact that he thought he was a better fighter than me. He was dismissive, that was it. That was what was making me angry. Fighters always have to think they're better than the guy they're going to fight, but Cro Cop, like Jérôme Le Banner, had considered me in a different class to him. I was just a chubby coconut with a decent chin and heavy hands, that's all he thought of me. That's what pissed me off.

Mirko had been easily the most successful K-1 fighter so far to move over to Pride, and he was tearing his way through the Pride heavyweight division. In fact, he'd torn off eight wins over his last nine Pride fights, with his only loss being a title fight against Fedor, and even then he'd been able to break the Russian's nose, toss him out of the ring, then lose on a wafer-thin decision.

Although I doubt he remembered Melbourne, I think Mirko sensed I had an issue with him. Before the fight he came up to me and said, 'Whatever happens, we are friends, Mark, yes?'

I had no problem with this; Pride and K-1 kept a very fraternal atmosphere and I was happy to maintain it. My relationship with Mirko could be whatever he wanted it to be – after I got out there and took his head off.

The fight was a pretty good one. I was concerned Mirko would be on his bike the whole fight, with me copping counters and head kicks while I chased him around the ring. There was a bit of that; I ate a few head kicks and I did have to stalk him a lot, but he stood in front of me enough and I tagged him in the head and body pretty regularly. He hit me with two axe-kicks in that fight – in wrestling shoes, no less – and I ended up under him at the end of the fight when I got jack of him running away for most of the round. I then launched an ill-advised jump-kick at him, but I did enough for the decision.

All of a sudden I was two for two against a couple of the MMA's biggest stars. I reckoned I was ready to go and get that big Russian's belt.

I fought again two months later, headlining again, but this time against an unknown MMA property in Yōsuke Nishijima, a well-liked Japanese boxer trying MMA for the first time. It might seem strange, for those unfamiliar with Japanese MMA, that an inexperienced guy (and one I outweighed by a good 30 kilograms) would be put up against someone who'd just taken out their number-one heavyweight contender, but that was the Japanese way. I was Nishijima's Yoshida in that regard.

Our fight started a little later than expected – after a fight between Mark Coleman and Maurício 'Shogun' Rua hosted a few uninvited guests (Wanderlei Silva, 'Ninja' Rua and Phil Baroni) – but at least the crowd was well and truly primed for me and Nishijima atop the card.

I hadn't trained since Cro Cop when I got into the ring but I knew I'd be able to dominate in whichever way I chose. This could have been a fight in which I took Nishijima to the ground and smushed him with elbows and ground-and-pound strikes, but that wasn't the kind of fighting I liked and it wasn't the kind of fighting my fans liked, either.

Nishijima is a very talented boxer so I ate a lot of punches in that fight, but I gave out even more. He fought like a warrior, but I slowed him down with heavy knees midway through the second round, so with his speed advantage gone, I battered him until he went to the floor after a left hook/straight right combination, and he didn't get back up.

I was getting a little run together in Pride, feeling like myself again. I was regaining faith in my hands and my ability to drop whomever they put in front of me.

Unbeknown to me, when I'd fought Mirko I was in a title eliminator. Whoever took that fight was to be fighting Fedor for the Pride belt. After the Nishijima fight I was called to a hotel suite, and when I saw the Russian champ coming out of the room as I was about to go in, I started to glean what was going on. I had a little chit-chat with Fedor in the hallway and asked him what they had for me.

He shrugged and said, 'They had this for me,' nodding to his bag.

When I got into the room I found Sakakibara-san, a few guys who looked like muscle and a Korean guy who acted like he was in charge. Also in the room was a table struggling under the weight of many giant piles of crisp currency, stacked neatly.

'How are you, Mark?' Sakakibara-san asked.

'I'd be doing better if I had some of that,' I said, pointing to the table.

'Do you want some? Would you like us to pay you in cash? We can if you like, Mark.'

No shit. They could have paid me for my next ten fights and it wouldn't have made a dent in that pile. I declined, though. The Russians all liked to be paid in cash but I figured it would be a pain trying to explain to Aussie Customs why I was bringing a big bag of foreign currency home.

In that hotel room I got a little preview of the future downfall of Pride, but at the time I didn't concern myself with any of the organisation's shady, behind-the-scenes dealings. I only concerned myself with the guy in front of me, and in that hotel suite they told me that soon the guy in front of me was going to be exactly the right bloke – the world's biggest badass. Well, second biggest anyway.

Before that fight Pride also asked me to fight in their first-ever Las Vegas card – part of a planned international expansion – against super heavyweight boxer

Eric 'Butterbean' Esch. I was more than happy to take the fight. Not only would it get me back to Vegas – a place where I could revel in my sins – but I'd also be fighting a bloke who would almost certainly stand with me.

Sadly visa issues put paid to that fight, with my visa coming through three days after the event. I watched Butterbean quickly finish Sean O'Haire from the third row, with Dana and Lorenzo sitting behind me.

Instead of the Butterbean fight, it was mandated that I should compete in a sixteen-man Pride open weight tournament. I won my first fight, stopping a bloodied but very game Tsuyoshi Kohsaka in the second round, but I put in a pretty sub-par performance in my semifinal against Josh Barnett.

After the Barnett fight I realised how much I still had to learn about professional MMA. I'd never had any problem dispelling fear or anger when I fought – during street fights I'd always fought to win so I fought effectively and dispassionately – and there was no way anyone was going to get me particularly riled or upset in a fight, but Josh managed to get me the other way. He's a funny dude, and he'd launched a charm arsenal in the lead-up to our fight. During the weigh-ins, during our press calls, even just moments before the bell rang, the jokes came thick and fast – but when the bell rang he was ready to fight and I was not.

That was a short fight. Barnett got on top of me quickly and locked me in a Kimura arm lock in less than five minutes, which forced me to tap or have my arm broken. As I walked back to the lockers I felt embarrassed and inexperienced. I'd slacked off working on my BJJ and ground game, and a bloke I should have knocked off had put me away pretty easily.

The greatest annoyance was I knew what I should have been doing, too. I decided to bring Steve Oliver over to live with me – I thought perhaps if he was hanging around the house I'd be shamed into training. It didn't work.

Steve is a great bloke and a great trainer, but having another authority figure in my new house wasn't ideal, especially considering what Steve's work involved. Like Sam Marsters and my father, Steve was going to be physically dominating me. I was a rich man on a successful MMA run. Having Steve in my home ordering me around just wasn't going to work.

At the time I believed that if I worked harder I could beat anyone in Pride, but I now realise there was another aspect of professional Japanese MMA that I hadn't embraced, which probably put me at a disadvantage. When I first met with Sakakibara-san and the Pride officials in Japan after signing my contract they gave me a rundown of the guidelines the company expected me to stay within, but there was no mention of performance-enhancing drugs. When I asked what the story was with PEDs, they laughed uniformly.

'Mark, you can take whatever you want,' one of them said.

When I first started kickboxing in Sydney, I'd seen the effects of the anabolic steroid Stanozolol on fighters. Their bodies changed, their power changed, but also their temperaments. I didn't want to mess with that stuff, mostly because I didn't think I had to. I never doubted that I had enough power to put anyone away but I thought PEDs could actually affect my timing and my countenance, which might make things harder for me.

Looking at the number of Pride fighters who've moved over to the UFC (where there are stricter rules) and either disappeared ignominiously or copped a suspension (or suspensions) for a banned substance, it's likely that the use of 'roids in Pride was pretty rampant, and there's little doubt that I fought against juiced opponents. Whatever the case, though, I lost in Pride because I was fucking around, not because I wasn't on the juice.

It was strange how wild and loose things could be in Japan. I remember one occasion when I'd broken my finger, I put a brace on my hand before I went to get it strapped.

The guy who did the strapping – the Japanese version of a commission official – said he wouldn't strap me with the brace on. I said I wasn't fighting without it, so there we were, at an impasse. When one of the Pride functionaries who kept things ticking over backstage came and asked if I was ready, I pointed out the impediment.

After a stern word I was strapped, and not just that, while I was walking to the ring I saw the reluctant official getting the shit beaten out of him by some sketchy-looking Japanese gangsters. That's just how it went at Pride.

My fight against Fedor was atop Pride's big 2006 NYE card, Pride Shockwave, again with 50,000 in attendance. I dominated the first seven minutes of the fight, which ended up running eight minutes. After clipping Fedor with a left hook in the initial exchanges, the Russian took the fight to the ground where, to everyone including my corner's surprise, I managed to take the top position. Eventually we got back on our feet before heading back to the ground again, and again I ended up in the advantageous position, going into a side mount.

At that point I'd never won a submission victory in MMA – in fact, I still haven't – and Fedor had never been submitted, but I tried twice to grab his arm and finish him with an arm lock. I got close, too. I hadn't really trained on submissions, I'd mostly just worked on escapes, but enough fighters had tried to put me in an arm lock for me to know how it worked. I got the hands in position, locked in his left arm, cranked it and . . . You know what, nearly getting a submission is like nearly winning the lottery: no one wants to hear about that shit.

I had two sub attempts and no joy – all I had to show for it was fatigue. Fedor dumped me on my back in the eighth minute and I was too shattered to defend myself properly. The Russian locked in his own arm lock and, on the first attempt, got me to tap. If there was one dude who knew how to finish a submission, it was Fedor.

After the fight, discontent set in. I'd lost and even though I was almost universally congratulated, I was embarrassed by how unprepared I'd been. I'd come so close to being recognised as the best fighter in the world, but I let that opportunity go because I was still being lazy.

I had a talent for scrapping and I'd never been bad with my hands, but that wrestling and BJJ, that stuff is a grind, and I hadn't embraced it yet. I'd carved out a lot of training time for ground fighting, displacing my striking or fitness stuff, but when the time came for a session I often blew it off, instead playing Counter-Strike or heading to the pub to play the pokies.

There was no other way around it, I'd been an asshole. As is often the case with me, when I'm pissed off with myself it channels itself somewhere – sometimes somewhere good, sometimes somewhere bad. After the Fedor loss I saw there was an opportunity for me to re-focus on my training. Like my first fights with Mirko and Jérôme, a rematch was going to be my motivation.

Fedor and I were among the biggest names in Pride at the time, so I knew our orbits would swing back to meet once again, sooner or later. When that happened, I was taking him out. His number was going to be punched. It was happening. I was going to get on that mat, get on that diet, lace up those running shoes and I was going to knock that big Russian blockhead off those shoulders.

Only that's not how it went down.

I'd never have that rematch with Fedor, and for a while it looked as though I might never beat anyone again. Trouble was coming, all kinds of trouble. Scandal was coming, and legal issues, and debt, and a forced exclusion from the sport. A baby was coming also, a son. It was the boy Julie and I had always wanted, but he didn't come into a happy house.

Darkness came over me, and rot. The spectre of my dead father would be cast over my house, and in the chill of his shadow I felt the possibility of my greatest and perhaps only real fear being realised – becoming like my dad.

Chapter 13

TOKYO, JAPAN
2008

I was living with Mark and I was eating what he was eating. Even though I couldn't get him to train, I was losing all kinds of weight. He hadn't shed a kilo. I went into his gaming room and said to him, 'You're a cheating motherfucker!' I grabbed the bin and found Twix wrappers and chips wrappers and all kinds of shit. I said, 'You've gotta tidy it up, bro. You're becoming a joke.' No matter who you are, on his best day, you'd be doing well to keep up with him, but Mark was just fucking around. He didn't know yet, but he had a fucking journey ahead of him.

STEVE OLIVER, TRAINER

When I heard rumblings of stories in the Japanese media about links between Pride and the *yakuza*, I thought nothing of it. I thought everyone knew what was going on – I didn't think it would be a surprise. I didn't think it would end up crippling the organisation and sending me into a spiral of debt, idleness and anger.

I never dreamed those media reports would take me to such a dark place. It's weird to think now that some enterprising Japanese journalism affected my life so significantly.

Let me explain. In professional *kakutougi* (roughly translated as 'spectacular combat sports' and shorthand for organisations like K-1 and Pride), the money was in free-to-air television rights. Not gambling or door tickets or endorsements or pay-per-view subscriptions or anything else, it was free-to-air TV.

The biggest live US television audience the UFC ever had was in 2011, when Cain Velasquez and Junior dos Santos fought for the heavyweight title in Anaheim, California, on Fox Sports. Around five and a half million viewers tuned in for that fight, but this was less than a third of the number of viewers Fuji TV regularly achieved with their Pride broadcasts.

Factor in the size of the Japanese population and, as a TV product, Pride was as big as baseball or basketball in the US or rugby league in Australia. Like K-1, Pride was a financial juggernaut propelled by a highly lucrative television deal. When that TV deal disappeared Pride was dead in the water.

It wasn't a lack of popularity that killed the Pride TV deal, but scandal. It all started when the weekly news magazine *Shūkan Gendai* ran a series of pieces about the ties between Pride's parent company, Dream Stage Entertainment, and a very powerful *yakuza* clan named the Yamaguchi-Gumi, which wasn't just one of the most powerful criminal organisations in Japan, but in the world.

The magazine pieces suggested that until 2003 the clan only had a very minor involvement with Dream Stage, in which they may have been collecting a small 'tax' at each event and infrequently arranging favourable outcomes for certain fights. After 2003, however, and specifically after the suspicious death of Naoto Morishita, the president of Dream Stage Entertainment, the magazine claimed that the Yamaguchi-Gumi had cut themselves into the real Pride money, the television money, and had became a partner of, if not the owner of, the organisation.

Shūkan Gendai ran reams of stories about Pride's supposed links to the *yakuza*, but the most damning was the reporting of a lawsuit that alleged ex-*yakuza* fixer and K-1 organiser Seiya Kawamata had been criminally extorted in 2003 by a man named 'Mr I' in the presence of a number of men, including Pride boss Sakakibara-san. Yep, the same man I'd threatened to chuck in Sydney Harbour.

This Mr I was later revealed to be Kim Dok-Soo, a man of Korean background who was a former loan shark and a high-ranking member of the Yamaguchi-Gumi. I'd bumped into him a number of times at Pride events and his importance in the organisation was obvious, if not his actual role.

My boys and I called him the 'Diamond Guy' because he liked to adorn himself with jewellery, and I remember one instance when I was coming out of a club and some of Mr I's boys were out the front waiting for him, and looking after a couple of Lamborghinis. Tooks and I were admiring the cars when Mr I came out and said something to his guys.

'You want to take a car, Hunto-san?' one of the guys asked.

'She's right, mate.' Nothing's free in this life.

Sakakibara-san claimed the allegations made by Kawamata-san were false and malicious, but nonetheless the fabric of the organisation began to unravel. Perhaps the last straw was when *Shūkan Gendai* revealed that Kunio Kiyohara, the Fuji TV producer in charge of the Pride broadcasts, not to mention son of the CEO of Fuji TV's parent company, was friendly with Yamaguchi-Gumi members and even lived in the same luxury apartment block as Mr I.

In June 2006 a lawyer from Fuji TV handed Sakakibara-san a termination notice, stating that the television company would no longer be showing Pride events. Furthermore, the company's contracted talent – like myself – were blacklisted and would no longer be welcome on any Fuji TV shows. I remember thinking it was a pity I wouldn't be able to do those Fuji shows anymore. I enjoyed my TV appearances in Japan, appearing on crazy game shows doing tug-of-war competitions or arm wrestling or whatever.

What I didn't understand at the time, though, was that this was an existential crisis for Pride. A multi-billion-yen company, Fuji TV was gouging out a cancer as far as they were concerned, and no new free-to-air TV company was going to take on the potential liability of a *yakuza*-run organisation that had been publicly discredited in the way Pride had.

Pride arranged for their planned events to be shown via pay-per-view, but the revenue from those buys was insignificant compared with the money Fuji TV had been paying them. Dream Stage Entertainment limped on for a few more months (and in those few months, that's when I fought Fedor) until they were acquired by Zuffa Inc., the parent company that owned the Ultimate Fighting Championship (UFC), which had recently (in fact, at the precise moment Sakakibara-san was handed the Fuji TV letter of termination) become the biggest and most profitable MMA organisation in the world.

When the UFC took over Pride I'd just signed a new deal with Pride, which still had a significant number of fights in it. UFC bosses Lorenzo Fertitta and Dana White came to Japan and held a large televised media conference in which they announced that Pride would continue to operate as it had been, with the Pride champions sometimes crossing over to fight the UFC champions in what White described as the 'Super Bowl of combat sports'.

American fans were excited at the prospect of Pride versus UFC competitions and I was happy to hear business would continue as normal. When I did finally get over Fedor, I was sure I wouldn't have any problems whupping whoever had the UFC belt at the time.

The Japanese fans, however, knew the prospect was doomed. The only way Pride could continue was with a free-to-air television deal, and there were simply too many impediments for that goal to be achievable.

The UFC planned to retain the managerial structure of Pride and while there was no legal proof of wrongdoings, the management team had lost face after the *Shūkan Gendai* articles. The overheads of the organisation had also become unmanageable and there were rumours of a great amount of shadowy debt hidden somewhere. Perhaps those issues could have been addressed, but the insurmountable problem was the fact that Pride was now owned by *gaijin*. After the deal, Pride was seen by the Japanese public only as an arm of the UFC, and they always had far less enthusiasm for American organisations than for homegrown products.

Zuffa finally admitted defeat in late 2007, with Dana declaring he and the company had done everything they could to arrange a new TV deal – but all they'd found was closed doors. They would have to shutter Pride.

While this all went on I proceeded to live as though I was going to earn the same as I had for the previous six years. With no fights on the horizon, my camp disbanded and for a while I stopped training altogether. I started gambling heavily again. There was a pub next to my house with a pokie room and staff who would sort me with free food and drinks, so I put tens, possibly hundreds of thousands of dollars through those machines.

In 2007 I decided to try my hand at promoting. When I signed my first Pride deal they also gave me naming rights to Pride events in Oceania. Even though those rights had now become worthless, I'd always liked the idea of hosting MMA events in Sydney and promoting the sport that had given me so much, so I started an organisation called the Oceania Fighting Championships.

My first port of call after I'd decided to mount an event was Lucy Tui, who had a skillset across match-making, promotion, sponsorship and every other aspect of fight event management. When I arrived at my first event at the Bonnyrigg Serbian Centre I felt a sense of accomplishment. It was only a few short years since I'd fought in that place, and not just that, losing, having been dropped by some unknown kickboxer after a day of sandblasting. Now I was returning as the promoter, having been to the very top of the martial arts mountain.

I hosted two events and they were really good ones, with good fighters and good fights. The stand-out fight was Cuban–Australian middleweight Hector Lombard's destruction of Fabio Galeb, whose performance was especially notable because he'd fought only a week earlier on a card in the Gold Coast.

Sakakibara-san and some of his business partners flew in just for the day to observe my second event, and I really appreciated their patronage and support. They praised me for the event, which was an operational success but, as it turned out, a financial failure.

In 2000 I used to set up chairs for Lucy's events, earning $50 cash in hand per event. In 2007 I found that setting up chairs was about $100,000 more lucrative than hosting events. Perhaps I was too used to the production values of Pride; perhaps I was just better at being in the ring than outside it, but either way those losses came at a particularly bad time.

I had other overheads, big ones. I had two mortgages, a lot of blokes had their hands in my pocket and I continued to live as though there were going to be more fights and more pay cheques. For many months after the sale of Pride I'd pester the UFC, asking when I was going to be fighting again. First I was told there'd be more Pride events soon, then I was told I was moving over to the UFC as one of the handful of Pride fighters who would be incorporated into the UFC roster.

Not long after that the response changed again: my services weren't needed. I was the odd man out. I didn't understand, I was a big draw and had just fought for the heavyweight title. I had a contract, for fuck's sake. It was a delicate situation which I still don't fully understand; even now there's a lot I can't say about the transition – but suffice it to say I was on the shelf and pissed about it.

Since I'd started fighting in Pride I'd been trying to reconnect with my children in Auckland. While my daughter wanted nothing to do with me and is still understandably angry with me, my son, Caleb, was starting to warm to the idea of his absent dad as a real person, not just a name.

When Caleb's mum called me and said he was twelve now, and was getting to that age where a paternal influence could be useful, I spoke to Julie about Caleb living with us. She thought it was a really good idea; we had this giant house and it seemed I'd be home a lot more in the immediate future. She thought it would be good for both me and the boy.

When Caleb arrived I didn't connect with him at all. I don't know why; perhaps it was because I just didn't know him, or how kids should be at his age. I was so adrift and so wild when I was a pre-teen that I just couldn't relate to Caleb and I certainly didn't know how to father him.

Even though we spoke about Caleb being my son and how important it was that I parent him, Julie ended up looking after him. I wasn't kind to the kid. It wasn't that I was cruel or violent or anything, but just moody, angry and stern. I was devastated when I found out Julie had been sending Caleb to his room when she knew I was coming home, just to make sure there wouldn't be a confrontation about Caleb leaving his socks on the floor or a bowl in the sink or whatever.

With no income and no desire to downsize my extravagant lifestyle, my financial situation got worse and worse.

I was offered a lucrative deal to wrestle on a New Japan professional wrestling card and I thought that was something I could do to stay solvent, but the legal advice I got on my contract was that I was locked out from doing any combat sports, including wrestling.

My situation grew more and more desperate and I had to take out more and more loans, until I finally got word, in 2008, that I was now allowed to take some fights elsewhere. My issue with my Pride contract hadn't been resolved, not yet, but I could at least get out there and fight in the meantime.

The obvious place for me was in Japan, with DREAM, a new MMA fighting organisation launched by some of the now-jobless executives who had worked on the Pride events. DREAM was owned by the Fighting and Entertainment Group, the parent company that also owned K-1, so the offer they brought to me was two-fold. DREAM had arranged a deal with a Russian fighting organisation, M-1, over rights to their biggest star and part owner, Fedor Emilianenko, allowing him to fight in Japan on their cards. Beating Fedor was something I was pretty keen on doing, but before I was going to get Fedor, they wanted me to go back and fight again for the K-1 title. That prospect didn't excite me at all.

I'd moved on from kickboxing and from K-1. My attitude in 2002 was that I'd already ticked that box, and by 2008 my attitude was, if anything, even more trenchant. My paymasters were insistent, though. The dominant force in K-1 was now the giant Dutchman Semmy Schilt, who had won the last three GP's, and had taken out Ernesto Hoost, Ray Sefo, Peter Aerts and my old mate Jérôme Le Banner in the process.

They were running out of bodies to throw at Schilt, who, at seven feet tall, had a range that was unmanageable for even the tallest fighters in the organisation. I would be a match for him, they thought, or at the very least I would be able to stand with him and trade leather.

When I walked into the Yokohama Arena to fight Schilt, my lack of training was obvious. I've always been a pretty stocky dude, but when I stepped into the ring for that fight I had legitimate love handles. I didn't want to be there, I hadn't trained and I didn't give a shit whether I won or lost, so of course I lost. I didn't actually have as many problems getting into Semmy's range as people thought I might, and I clocked him with a few stiff leaping overhand rights. I didn't have the fitness to follow up those punches, though, and I couldn't get away from the big Dutchman's Dhalsim-like kicks. Semmy got me in the guts with a spinning back-kick at the end of the first round and I couldn't answer the bell for the second. That was my last K-1 fight.

In the larger scale of things I didn't care too much about that loss. Of course I was never happy about being stopped in a fight, but I didn't consider myself a K-1 fighter anymore, I was an MMA guy.

My first fight in DREAM was to be in Osaka against Sergei Kharitonov, a Russian fighter with an impressive record but, at the last minute, he pulled out and was replaced by Dutch kickboxer-cum-MMA-wunderkind Alistair Overeem, who'd won his first fight at nineteen and even though he was seven years younger than me, he'd had thirty more professional MMA fights.

Again, I rolled into that fight fat. I weighed in about ten kilograms heavier than the UFC heavyweight limit and I was also pretty unfit. I still fully expected to beat Overeem, however. Three days before the fight the guy had been on a beach in Thailand, not expecting to fight for some months, and only just got to Osaka in time to weigh in.

In the opening exchange of the fight I pushed the Dutchman over and as he fell I jumped onto him on the ground, quickly moving to side control. On the ground, though, I was at sea. I'd been shirking my training with Steve and BJJ wasn't like stand-up fighting, which was as natural to me as breathing. I had no instincts, no power and no stamina. Even when I fought Yoshida in my first MMA fight I had my natural ability to guide me and my kickboxing strength and fitness, but in this fight I felt like a little kid again, powerless and shamed. Overeem quickly locked his legs around my arm and rolled me for an arm bar finish. It was the shortest fight of my MMA career so far.

When I got home I was filled with frustration. I'd lost three consecutive fights – four if you count the K-1 bout – and that was something new for me. It wasn't the sting of defeat fuelling my frustration, though, it was my inability to do anything about it. For some reason, I couldn't bring myself to train properly and I couldn't bring myself to eat properly. I couldn't stop smoking and drinking. I was going backwards financially, also something I couldn't seem to do anything about. Spending as I was, I now needed to fight, which hadn't been the case for me since I won the GP. If I sustained one significant injury I'd be in a ruinous situation.

When I walked into my giant house I no longer felt a sense of satisfaction, only the weight of all the mortgages I'd accrued. Debt hung around my neck like a millstone. Debt had been one of the things that had wrecked my father. Debt was wrecking me.

The next event that took place would bring both pressure and immense joy into my life – my son Noah was born. I was there for that one, down at Liverpool Hospital. When he emerged, tiny and helpless, I felt nothing but happiness and love for the little bundle.

Later I would feel the strain of having another dependant, but on the day he was born I was calm and happy. I knew that because of his mother. In many ways Julie had raised me, but by the time she got to me I already had some fucked-up habits. Still, I think she did a pretty good job with me, and regardless of what was happening with this little dude's dad, he would always have a rock-solid mum.

When I was told my next fight was against Le Banner, I thought maybe my fortunes had turned. Jérôme had taken MMA fights on and off since I'd beaten him in the GP in 2001 but he hadn't faced the kind of opponents I'd faced, and I had no doubt I was going to take him out.

When Jérôme dropped out and they replaced him with journeyman middleweight Melvin Manhoef, again on short notice, I knew I was assured victory. Manhoef stood only about five foot seven, and would weigh in a good 40 kilograms lighter than me. I'd be able to bully him on the ground, throw him around in Thai clinches and bludgeon my fists straight through his standing defence. There was no way he could possibly beat me. Perhaps DREAM knew that too. Perhaps they wanted to protect their asset.

The fight was on a giant 2008 New Year's Eve card, with eighteen bouts and some of the biggest names from both

DREAM and K-1 fighting. It felt good to be walking back into the Saitama Super Arena knowing that I was going to get my arm raised. Pride comes before a fall, though. That fight would be the worst loss of my career. I know I'll never have another like it.

He's muscular, Melvin, but he still looked like a child in front of me when we were called to fight. I was anxious to get it all over and done with.

'READY? FIGHT!' the ref called.

I pivoted around the middle of the ring while Melvin danced, then I came at him with a long right and a left, and then . . . and then?

They were bright, those lights.

I have a fight soon. I need to open my eyes. I have a fight soon. I'm fighting. Who am I fighting? Who is this guy? What's that noise? I have to fight soon. I have to get up. GET UP.

Man, those lights were so bright. I'd never been knocked out cold before. I'd been fighting my whole life and against giants of men, but I'd never been laid out like that. It was only when my eyes came into focus and I saw Melvin dancing around like a maniac that I realised what had happened.

When I was backstage showering, my mind was on a strange feedback loop. I kept thinking the fight hadn't happened yet, until I would see those lights and remember it was all over. The fight was over, and maybe my fighting career. Who could I possibly beat, if not this little bloke?

I'd bested the best at K-1 and climbed pretty close to the top of the mountain in Pride. I believed I had a gift. I thought I was the best fighter on the planet and that faith had been hard to shake even after a run of losses. Now, however, I had a crisis in faith.

When I got back home I didn't know what to do with myself. While I was winning I didn't have to think about anything else in life besides putting hands on people. I had no money problems and no children, but that had all changed.

When Noah was born it was a day that can't be compared to any others, and he is and always will be a ray of light through the darkest days, but when I came back from being knocked out by Melvin I saw him and I just felt panic. There weren't going to be any more paydays if I kept losing, and if I couldn't beat Melvin, who could I beat?

For the first time since I was a little kid I felt stuck, hemmed in by my circumstances. As had been the case when I was young I couldn't bring myself to do anything about it except rage at the world around me.

I thought about debt a lot and, in a great paradox, it seemed the only way I could stop thinking about it was by gambling. I was training infrequently, if at all, eating like a lard-ass, gambling like a maniac and generally treating the people around me like shit, and I just couldn't stop any of it. That frustration I recognised.

I'd never understood the cruelty of my father until I was staring at a future that was going to be far more difficult than I'd imagined. I had anger in me; I had always had volcanic anger in me, but for much of my adult life that anger was dormant. Now it started spilling over, spitting and frothing with burning heat.

There was danger for those around me, but all I could see was my own fury. More and more I took my anger out on Caleb. That boy had really started loving his dad. Yes I'd been absent, but in my absence I'd done the things South Aucklanders admired most. I was famous, and famous for being the toughest man in the toughest sport. What red-blooded part-Samoan near-teen Kiwi boy wouldn't love that? I found it hard to reciprocate his love, though. I was happy to be mates with him but I fucked up any time I tried to be a father.

With my kids now, I'm always thinking about them and what's best for them – that's the only thing I've had a stronger instinct for than fighting – but with Caleb, he landed in my life already his own person. I just couldn't relate to him. I couldn't be consistent with him. I'd have to force myself to treat him the way he should be treated, and if you're a parent you know that's not going to work. I was bad at disciplining him because I was ruled by my moods, and my moods were getting shittier and shittier.

I was never physical with Caleb, or Julie or anyone in my house, but I certainly raged inside that house and I was a physical menace outside my own door. I was becoming an ogre – a dangerous, rage-filled man free of joy or empathy or compassion. There was a rot in me that was growing. It was eating my life, destroying my family and killing my career. I had to do something about it.

An American MMA fighter named James Lee, who had stayed with me while he trained in Sydney, extended an invitation to train with him in his native Detroit. That would be something different, maybe the something different I needed, so I packed my bags and flew east.

In Detroit I trained with James during the day and at night we went from bar to bar. I enjoyed the training and loved the city, which was grand but also real and working class, but the experience didn't end up helping me in the ring.

After three years in my house, Caleb had left and gone home to his mother while I was in Detroit. Apparently I could be absent or angry, but not at the same time. Poor bastard, I can't imagine what it must have been like living with me at that time.

I rolled into my last DREAM fight with a head full of mess. For a good chunk of my life the ring would be the place where I felt most comfortable, a place where I could clear my mind and let God move through me, but I went into that last fight tight, angry and, yet again, woefully underprepared.

The fight was the quarterfinal of the DREAM SuperHulk tournament, which had the same format as the Pride tournaments but neither the prestige nor the talent. The fighters in the tournament would include Bob Sapp, who was about to go 1–16 in his next seventeen fights; Hong Man Choi, a seven-foot-two Korean who moved like a tectonic plate; and even Jose Canseco, a confessed habitual steroid abuser and one of America's most maligned baseballers in his only ever MMA fight.

I was paired against 23-year-old Dutch–Iranian middleweight Gegard Mousasi. He was talented, but small, and he was another guy I should have beaten easily. He was another guy I lost to. It took a little more than a minute for him – maybe 95 kilograms – to get me – 135 kilograms – on my back. Like many before him Gegard snaked in an arm bar easily, forcing me to tap. When I did, I knew I'd reached the end of the line.

My DREAM career, which had totalled less than three fighting minutes, was over. I was supposed to fight two more times in that organisation, but they were done with me. Hong Man Choi and Bob Sapp were still welcome in DREAM, but my services were no longer needed.

Pride was gone, the DREAM and K-1 doors had closed and I was on a six-fight losing streak. I was fucked, I was well and truly fucked. I really had something to be angry about then.

Chapter 14

TOKYO, JAPAN
2013

Back in Japan there was a lot of shady stuff going on,
like managers who were getting paid by the promoters to
keep the fighters in the dark and underpaid. When I saw
that Mark had landed on his feet in the UFC, I was happy
to see it. He was always one of the good ones. I was
hoping he'd end up fighting Mirko, and beating the shit
out of him, but you can't have everything you want.

MIRO MIJATOVIC

It all came to a head one day in 2010. I was in a video
games retailer on Campbelltown's main street with Julie
and the baby looking for a new PlayStation game to play
when a man saw me from the street and came at me. He
wasn't a big guy and he didn't look like a tough guy, either,

but he made a beeline for me, bumping into me deliberately and staring me down.

I gave him that old stare. That South Auckland stare.

'You wanna come outside?' he asked. The guy was twitchy, maybe even druggy.

I followed him out and a moment after he raised his hands the guy was unconscious, lying in a pool of his own blood. I walked away quickly as people gathered. I passed an ambulance with its sirens singing, rushing towards the store. I felt nothing. I felt no exhilaration, or anger, or hate, or even regret. I was simply neutral.

When I was a few blocks away I phoned Julie and told her where I was so she could come and pick me up. She was in tears.

'No Mark, I can't handle this anymore. You're on your own. I'm not coming.'

This wasn't the first such incident. A few months earlier I'd been involved in a bit of a road rage incident, with Julie and Noah once again in tow. Two men in a car had tailgated me, so I slowed deliberately. They raced ahead of me and parked in front of me at the lights. One got out of the car with his tyre iron as abuse was hurled to and fro. The other guy ended up under the wheels of his car, twitching with his eyes rolled back. I thought he was dying.

When the police arrived I was put in cuffs and taken to jail. After they'd interviewed the witnesses at the scene the police found I had no culpability under the law, but that didn't mean I was without sin. I couldn't simply walk away from a tense situation. All those little incidents in life that can spark anger between people were setting off a wildfire in me. I was dangerous again.

'I'm not coming to get you. I won't see you in prison. You need to sort yourself out or I'm leaving you, Mark,' Julie said after the Campbelltown incident.

There was now only a thin membrane of principles holding back the violent madness of my youth. I couldn't become that boy again; I couldn't give in to those old demons. I had a wife, a child and beyond that, my fists were too dangerous to be let loose. Perhaps they'd become ineffectual in the ring, but they could be lethal on the streets.

If I didn't get my shit together, Julie really was leaving me. She met me when I was a broke, wild, damaged kid who didn't understand why the sheets on a bed needed to be changed. She'd gone through the drugs and the gambling, not to mention the giant hole of distrust in my heart that needed to be filled in before I could marry. She'd gone through it all, but she couldn't stomach the anger. That was too much.

I desperately wished I could turn off the rage inside me, but it seemed the fuel for this anger in me was almost every aspect of daily life. I needed help.

The day after the Campbelltown incident I went to our GP and told him what had happened. He sorted me out with a referral for some counselling sessions, which I held as though it was covered in dog shit.

I knew Victoria had had counselling that had really helped her, but I wasn't Victoria. I wasn't big on strangers and I wasn't big on sharing, but I didn't have any choice – Julie wasn't big on empty proclamations.

I dragged myself to the first session by necessity, but as soon as we started talking I could feel the rot in me being slowly washed away. It was like those days back in Surry Hills when I used to lie on my bed and tell Julie about what life was like when I was kid.

The counsellor was an intelligent, softly spoken African woman, and I reckon she got into the meat of me pretty quickly. I told her some pieces of my personal history – just grabs here and there – but I could tell she was picking up the rest. She was good at what she did, and could see the scars inside me.

When I left my first session I was actually looking forward to going back. Each session brought relief, like air being let out of a balloon that was fit to burst. I reckon she told me more about myself than I'd told her about me.

I realised I was naturally generous and trusting, but could become bitterly resentful any time I felt that trust had been breached. The breaking points of my trust were irregular, too. In some instances, people leeched money off me for years without me ever noticing. In others there were innocent, misconstrued words spoken to me that I harboured in my memory for years like a death vendetta.

It all went back to that house. Of course it did. I started life trapped in a house that was vicious. When I felt trapped again, I reverted to viciousness. Dog eat dog. Rage first, think later.

My counsellor not only dug into the source of my anger, but gave me some little ways to stay cool when something started to heat me up. The guys who cut me off, that bloke who shoved me in the bakery queue, the dude whose elbow keeps banging mine on the plane's armrest; they might be having the worst day in the world. They might have just been given a nasty medical diagnosis; their wives might have just left them; hell, some of them might have even had a worse childhood than mine. Who knows? I suppose the key to keeping myself on an even keel boiled down to the simplest mantra – everybody hurts. There were so many times those sessions directly helped me.

We'd moved from my mansion in Oakdale to a smaller, but still very large place in Denham Court, but even then ended up defaulting three times on the mortgage. The sheriff came to the house to let us know it was to be repossessed, and I found out about it while I was overseas training, with a crying wife and screaming baby down the line.

My instinct was to feel the fury and fight tooth and nail to save the place. I could have rushed back and created a scene when next a Sheriff or, God forbid, a banker came to my house looking for the keys. On a less extreme level, I suppose I could have leveraged a rental property and a small personal gym that I owned outright, and tried to stay afloat that way, but I did neither. I sold the Denham Court place and downsized to a humbler place in which Julie is a hell of a lot happier. It was the right thing to do, the wise thing to do.

I also credit, in no small part, those counselling sessions for my success in the UFC. My training turned around after those sessions. Looking back, it might even be possible that I stopped training when I started losing so I could maintain the idea that I was the best fighter in the world. I could say to myself, *Of course I lost, I wasn't training.* But more than that, I might not even be in the UFC without that counselling.

Like I said before, I'm not at liberty to say what happened after Pride was dissolved and Zuffa picked up my contract, but I can say that I was very angry about the situation. As far as I was concerned, the UFC were trying to put their hand in my pocket, but the situation was a lot more complex than that.

At the time I cursed those three letters, U-F-C, and when they offered me a three-fight contract I wanted to tell them to shove it up their fucking asses. I couldn't be talked down, either. Even though I had a baby and wife to support and a latent desire to get back atop the MMA pile, I was willing to cut that nose right off my face – if keeping the nose meant working with the UFC.

I harboured secret thoughts of taking their contract and walking into the Octagon for my first fight, throwing in the towel and walking straight out again. I thank God I realised I was being an asshole. It took me a while to change my mind about fighting in the UFC, and it wasn't the earning potential that did it, it was the idea of taking that belt.

I know it must seem odd for a guy in his mid-thirties on an epic losing streak, with some of those losses coming from middleweights, but I never really believed anyone in the world was a better fighter than me and, by then, all of the best fighters in the world were slowly but surely being collected in one place.

I agreed to the terms and signed up. I had a new fighting lease and I still felt I had some power left in me. I thought if I trained hard, I could still get past guys like Fedor and Mirko.

After the DREAM nightmare, my entire camp had disappeared. When I signed with the UFC, the first guy I called was Steve Oliver. 'I'm going over to the UFC, and this is my last chance. This is going to be weird, because you've kind of been training me for years, but . . .'

'What, you really want to train now?' Steve said.

'Yeah. It's now or never. I really need to do this right.'

Steve Oliver comes from a long line of professional trainers, and although he swears like a sailor and is a big, tattooed unit, he puts the art in martial arts. He's a bloke who takes sabbaticals around the world to study different disciplines and has black belts in many of them. Unlike some of the others who have cornered for me over the years, Steve wasn't in it for the money and fun, he was in it for professional reasons. He was in it because martial arts were his passion.

He was always disappointed when I lost, mostly because he thought I could be something special. I'd barely trained with Steve during my DREAM 'career' but now he agreed to get on this ride to see how far it could go. I'd been a lazy fucker, though, and most people would have given up on me.

'Fuck Mark, I've been waiting for this call for years,' Steve said. 'Of course mate, let's fuckin' do this thing.'

I knew I needed Steve in my corner, but I also decided one of the few things I did right while I was on my DREAM losing slump was taking my camp offshore. It was too hard to have my training and my family in close proximity. On Steve's recommendation we moved over to train for my first UFC fight at American Top Team (ATT), a large MMA camp in Florida founded by Brazilians Ricardo Liborio and Marcus 'Conan' Silveira.

Both Ricardo and Conan were BJJ black belts and ground-fighting experts, and their camp was full of veteran fighters who knew their MMA, including some of the top talents in the UFC and some particularly tall fighters, which would be useful for me against the undefeated six-foot-seven giant Sean 'Big Sexy' McCorkle, my first UFC opponent.

It was when I arrived in Indianapolis for that first fight that I realised how far my stock had fallen. In Japan I'd been a rock star. My face was on billboards and playing cards, I was mobbed on the street and celebrities surreptitiously asked me out on dates. When I got to Indiana, I was just another fighter at just another event in a city that would pay attention to fighting for just a few days.

For the first time in my career I experienced what life was like for the journeyman fighters. Where the Japanese organisations had laid out plush red carpets for my camp – who often got their own rooms, drivers and per diems – the UFC gave me one hotel room, a shuttle to the arena and that was pretty much it.

It had felt like only days before that I was headlining events at the 50,000-seat Saitama Super Arena. Now I was on the bottom of an eleven-fight card. The most galling fact was that atop that card was Mirko, who'd managed to carve himself a pretty impressive UFC career since the dissolution of Pride.

I went into that first fight the best fighter I'd been in years, but it still only took a minute or so to be beaten again. As soon as we touched gloves, McCorkle wrapped himself around me, looking for the takedown. He was even happy for me to be on top, as it only took him a very short amount of time to sweep past me, take one of my arms and lock it in for yet another fucking arm bar.

I tried to hold off on tapping, but the pressure built and built until my elbow hyper-extended and popped out. The ref jumped in and called it. I'd lost again.

When I heard the announcer Bruce Buffer saying, '. . . at one minute, three seconds of the very first round . . .' I could scarcely believe it. I'd trained for this fight. I thought I was in good shape, but here it was, yet another submission loss. And this time it wasn't against Fedor, but a UFC debutant right at the bottom of the toilet card. I thought I was starting my UFC career at the bottom, but after that loss, I found that there were even more depths to plumb.

After the McCorkle fight the UFC tried to dissolve my contract, claiming it was too dangerous for me to fight in their organisation. That was the ultimate ignominy. They weren't just saying I wasn't good enough, but that I could endanger myself by fighting in the Octagon. Eventually they relented and let me stay in the promotion, but I think only because the UFC was returning to my hometown of Sydney for their second event and they had very few local fighters to put on the card.

The guy I fought in Sydney was, on paper, possibly the worst MMA fighter I've ever faced, in a fight that wasn't even on the undercard, but carried out pre-broadcast to have in the can just in case the broadcast went short. Despite the inauspicious circumstances I still consider it one of my greatest victories.

The fight started at ten in the morning, with people still filing into the stadium holding coffees and bacon and egg rolls. Most of the floor seats were empty as I walked in, but despite this, it was the warmest reception I'd had in my career. My last fight in Australia had been more than a decade earlier – against Ernesto Hoost in Melbourne – and while the Japanese were numerous and supportive in their own way, they couldn't compare to a stadium of Aussies cheering on one of their guys.

I had fewer mates at that fight than I did for most of my fights in Japan, but as I walked to the Octagon the crowd let me know I was home. Normally when I'm walking towards a fight I feel completely neutral, but in Sydney I had to remind myself to bottle my excitement.

I'd heard about the dangers of adrenaline dumping, but I never really understood it until the Sydney crowd roared after Bruce Buffer hollered my name.

'Fighting out of Sydney, Australia . . . Mark "Super Samoan" Hunt!'

In that moment I loved every single bastard in the place.

My opponent was Chris 'The Crowbar' Tuchscherer, an American wrestler in the Dan Bobish mould and a training partner of former heavyweight champion Brock Lesnar. Like me, Tuchscherer was in a precarious position with the UFC after a couple of losses. With both of us the wrong side of 35, it was pretty obvious this was a 'win or leave town' contest.

I managed to clip Tuchscherer a few times in the opening exchanges and caught him with a one–two combination that sent him to the canvas. There was a roar when the American fell, and had it been just a few years earlier I would have dived at him, but I was playing the game far more warily now.

C'mon boy, get back up. Let's go again.

Throughout that round I managed to tag Chris almost with impunity, giving him a mouse below his left eye and a large cut above until, with two minutes left in the first round, the ref jumped in to check if the American could continue.

'There's something in my eye,' Tuchscherer told the ref.

'Yeah, it's your eyelid,' the ref replied.

The doctors came over to check on Tuchscherer, telling him he should probably retire, but gave him the option of going on if he wanted to. Of course he wanted to. This dude's career was on the line. As soon as we were called back on, the newly energised Tuchscherer dived in for a takedown and he managed to get me on my back.

I guess he must have figured then that his only shot left was a submission – any more time on his feet and he was going to be stopped by either the doctors or me. From the top, Tuchscherer was pouring pints of his blood over me from the cut above his eye while he tried to lock in one of my arms for a submission.

With his blood lubing both of us up, it would have been hard to get that submission position, but he did manage it. There was a concerned groan as Tuchscherer grabbed my arm and twisted it for a Kimura, the position that had been my downfall so many times.

I thought for a moment that was going to be it until, honestly, the crowd gave me the energy to break that lock. They roared like I'd just won the State of Origin when I freed my arm.

These dudes were with me. It felt great. Tuchscherer stayed on top for the rest of the round but he didn't get another submission chance. When I walked to my corner I couldn't wait to get back into the middle. I was going to be stopping this shit.

We got back onto our feet and a battered Tuchscherer ran at my front leg, but he was too slow by then and I easily dived away. I was having fun now. This guy was ready to go out; I just had to wait for my spot.

I felt young again. I felt like me again.

I tagged Tuchscherer with glancing blow after glancing blow until I caught him with a crisp little uppercut on the jaw. As I felt the resistance go down my arm I knew he was out. There was no need to jump on him; this dinner was done.

I hadn't won a fight in five years, so raising my hands in a stadium full(ish) of my adopted countrymen felt joyous. As my arm was raised, I couldn't wait for the last fight of my contract. I'd win it, of that there was no doubt.

The last fight of the contract was to be against Ben Rothwell at the Pepsi Center in Denver. As I'd done in Indiana, I took off to American Top Team for my camp, but when I arrived there I found that a lot of the good heavyweights had scarpered after an argument over money. Without good sparring partners, I really had to look elsewhere.

Two weeks before the fight, I called up my buddy Jamie Te Huna, who was fighting on the same card, to ask if I could move to the MusclePharm gym in Denver where he was training with the Wolf Lair team and their star fighter, Quinton 'Rampage' Jackson. At MusclePharm I sparred primarily with Cheick Kongo, a muscle-bound Frenchman of African decent, and as soon as we started working I realised those sessions were going to be invaluable. Denver sits more than one and a half kilometres above sea level, and for big boys like me the thin air at that altitude is not much of a meal for hungry lungs.

I managed to get some good shots into Rothwell's jaw and eye during the fight, but that's not how I won it. I won it by sheer bloody perseverance. I didn't stop going forward, didn't stop throwing shots and I used my escapes, which I was now drilling more than anything else, to great effect.

The way I worked on my ground game had significantly changed by the time I got to the Rothwell fight. For a while my guys had tried to turn me into a useful BJJ fighter, but by Denver we realised it would be much more prudent just to concentrate on the four escapes which, if done properly, would get me back up on my feet.

As Bruce Lee once said, he didn't fear the man who had practised 10,000 kicks once, but the man who had practised one kick 10,000 times. I must have drilled those four escapes at least 10,000 times by then.

In the third round it looked as though we were both taking each breath through a straw, but I could tell by looking at Rothwell that the diameter of his straw was just that little bit smaller than mine. By the time I had my hand raised, Rothwell was exhausted, beaten and bloodied. I was exceptionally proud of my work. Of his last seventeen MMA fights, Rothwell had only lost twice – against Cain Velasquez and Andrei Arlovski. Rothwell was a fighter, an athlete and a talent, and I'd got over him through sheer bloody hard work.

Backstage I got a visit from Dana White. Things weren't ever really acrimonious between the two of us, but we were certainly at loggerheads over particular issues so I appreciated the visit. He'd come to apologise for how things had played out and to congratulate me personally for my performance.

There'd been another heavyweight fight on that main card – between Travis Browne and Rob Broughton – which had ended with booing. It's not easy for heavyweights to keep their pace up at altitude, and Dana had loved the way I'd managed it.

He had also come to invite me to the post-fight media conference – an honour usually reserved for the main and co-main event fighters and the finishing bonus winners. It was then that I knew my contract was going to be re-upped. I was in the UFC to stay.

My next deal, however, was to be the worst I'd signed in a decade. I still took it happily. My new manager told me it was the best I was going to get, and I believed him. The days of seemingly endless largesse were over. It was time to grind.

The part of the deal I especially liked was the generous monetary incentive for me to win. That was exactly what I was planning on doing: winning. I'd almost forgotten how good it was to win, how that feeling can flow through every minute of every day.

I was going for that UFC belt. People would have laughed if I'd said I was heading for the belt when I joined, so I didn't tell anybody. People would have laughed then too, but that was always the goal in my head. I now had six extra fights to set down that path. I needed the belt before it was all over. I still believed I had a gift given to me by God himself; I'd neglected it for so many years, but it hadn't left me.

No one can give a gift like this but God and I had to respect it in the same way I respected my other gifts, Julie and Noah. After that fight another gift came along. Julie and I hadn't had an easy time falling pregnant and we felt nothing less than blessed when a baby girl, Sierra, joined the brood.

Shortly after my baby girl's birth the UFC sent over a big box of kids' gear and a personal card addressed to Julie and me from Dana. That gesture meant a lot to me. I'd had quite a few teething problems with the UFC, which was a world away from the excesses and luxury of Pride and K-1. Indiana had been a shock, but after Denver I was ready to embrace the blue-collar journey I'd started with these guys. If I wanted excess, I would have to earn it.

My next UFC fight took me back to Japan. Apart from some early shows in rooms that weren't much bigger than scout halls, the UFC had never really tried to crack the Japanese market. With Pride gone, in 2012 it was time.

They arranged a stacked card for the event at the Saitama Super Arena, with fights involving most of the top contracted Japanese fighters, the two best lightweight fighters in the world scrapping for the title, and two of the few Pride guys left in the organisation, namely Rampage and myself.

My fight was against one of the dudes in the division I categorically didn't want to fight – not because I was concerned with him battering me, but because I was concerned with battering him. That fighter was Cheick Kongo. Cheick had helped me a lot in training for my must-win fight against Rothwell. I had no desire to put him away, but I knew why the fight made sense in UFC matchmaker Joe Silva's mind. Kongo was on a bit of a tear, too, and besides that, he looked like he was carved out of stone, something the Japanese fans would probably appreciate.

I knew I'd be able to put Kongo away. He was a striker, like me, with a background in karate, *kendo* and *savate* and he was someone who was going to stand and punch with me. Anyone who was going to stand and punch with me was going away.

I trained with Steve in my private gym near my house for the fight and when I travelled to Japan, I knew I was ready. I was strong and fit and my head was screwed on right.

I didn't relish fighting Kongo, but it was great to be back in Japan and at the Saitama Super Arena. When I'd last left that place it was with a sore jaw and a shattered ego, after the Melvin Manhoef fight. Back then I didn't know if I would ever get there again.

I dropped Kongo first with a left hook. The big Frenchman's knees buckled but I let him regain his posture – my days of jumping into my opponents' guard were over. He wobbled around for another 30 seconds or so, until I got him with a right that sent him semi-conscious and into the cage. I swarmed on him after and threw short right hooks until referee Herb Dean jumped in and saved him.

I got away clean in that fight. Kongo barely even had the opportunity to put a hand on me, so the UFC offered me a quick turnaround, which I very much appreciated. I did feel like I was in a bit of a hurry. My next fight was to be in Vegas against Dutch fighter Stefan Struve, whom they called 'Skyscraper' because of his seven-foot frame. This fight was part of an all-heavyweight card, with champion Junior dos Santos defending his belt against submission specialist Frank Mir in the main event. Shit was going to be settled on this card. If I could bust Struve up in a spectacular fashion, then tongues would start wagging.

Then, a week away from the fight, the posterior cruciate ligament (PCL) in my knee gave up. I was training at ATT in Florida when it happened, with my leg curling up involuntarily after a loud snap. I was taken away for X-rays and the doctor told me I needed surgery. I asked him if I could do it after the fight, and he told me that I literally had no PCL left. It was the ghost of K-1 past popping up again – Le Banner was looking to get one more stoppage against me.

I thought I could probably still walk on that leg if I had to, so I told my coaches I wanted to postpone the surgery and fight on. I'd never in my career turned down a fight. No training, injured, unfit – whatever, I was here to fight. Any man, any day was my fight philosophy.

Steve told me off for being stupid. 'Mate, you're being a fucking idiot,' he said. 'Struve's going to bring everything, and you're wanting to fight on one leg? That cunt's seven foot tall! How are you going to hit him with your stubby little fuckin' arms without being able to move?' It always bothered me how much Steve swears.

He was right, though. I was taking this stuff seriously now and it was pretty unlikely I could beat Struve with one leg. I was gaining a bit of momentum at the UFC so if I lost to him, a top-ten heavyweight, I'd get bumped down the back of the queue quite a bit. I had to think about this stuff strategically now: I knew I only had a limited number of years left in the cage, so I flew back to Sydney and went under the knife.

While I was recovering from surgery Struve beat his replacement opponent Lavar Johnson and also up-and-coming American–Croatian fighter Stipe Miočić. When they rescheduled my fight with Struve, now to be held in the Saitama Super Arena, he was an even bigger scalp.

I brought in a six-foot-eight Brazilian fighter named Marco 'Gigante' Villela, who got his BJJ black belt under Carlos Gracie Jr, to train with me so I could at least try to emulate the BJJ game of the Skyscraper, who had four submission wins on his UFC record. It was a chore, ground-fighting such a big bloke. I felt like I'd been stuffed in a sack full of wet ropes, but that was the job and I was up for it. By the time I got to Japan I was confident those big arms and legs of Struve's wouldn't be able to snake around my arms, legs or throat.

It was an odd fight. Struve is a full foot taller than me and I literally had to jump up with my left hooks to hit him in the face, but I did manage to land a few good ones in the first round. At every opportunity Struve would try to suck me back onto the ground and attempt to wrap one of his python-like arms or legs around me, but by then my escapes were working well. When I did end up on the ground it would only be for a few moments and I always managed to get myself back up again without too much damage having been inflicted.

It was a gruelling fight, but late in the third round I was able to hurt Struve with a left hook counter. While he stumbled backwards I tagged him again, this time a right on the forehead followed up by a running left hook that dropped him like a crash test dummy. Struve buckled against the cage after that punch. He was still conscious, but I knew it was over. I felt it down my arm. He was toast.

I started walking away, until I realised referee Herb Dean hadn't called it yet – in fact he was calling for Struve to stand back up again.

Really, dude?

I walked back to the broken Dutchman with my fists balling again, but Dean stepped in before I could put any more hurt on him. Just as well, too, as later Struve tweeted an X-ray that showed a jaw so broken you could put your little finger through it.

I was battered and exhausted, but I was back, man. I was back.

Chapter 15

TOKYO, JAPAN
2014

> He proved us wrong, he proved everybody who
> doubted him wrong. I think [Mark's] one of the
> greatest stories in sports right now.
> **DANA WHITE, UFC PRESIDENT**

Of us Hunt kids, John was the angry one, the brooding and quiet one. He was as smart as a whip, but his swinging moods were as unpredictable as autumn weather. From his mid-teens onwards there were long stretches when he lived like a hermit, shutting himself into his room for days on end, sometimes emerging with channelled purpose. He never explained to us what he was up to, or his reasoning; we'd just have to wait and watch to see what he was going to do. Then we'd deal with the results.

One day, shortly after I got out of prison for the first time, John had apparently resolved to belt the old man. We were all going about our day, then seemingly from nowhere, CRACK, a big shot to the old man's jaw. Dad was out for the count and I had to carry his fat ass to the hospital.

I never asked John why he belted the old man and I never asked him why he tried to kill himself, either. We never talked like that. No one talked with John like that.

Victoria ended up speaking to counsellors, I spoke to Julie, and even Steve yelled at the sky when he had to. John, though, he never shared. He kept all his hurt to himself. I suspect his deepest fears and most bitter hatreds stayed in his head, penned in by high walls. There they festered and became toxic.

It was after the Kongo fight that John first tried to commit suicide, at the house I bought for my folks. Victoria, John and Steve were all living in that place then, along with Vic's kids, whom John loved as though they were his own.

That day John came back from work whistling and seemingly happy. He went into the small room next to the kitchen, lay down a tarp, stacked his shoes on top of each other so they could serve as a pillow, grabbed a kitchen knife and stabbed himself in the chest and neck. When that knife broke, he went and got another one. John went under but not all the way, and was revived and taken to hospital.

When Vic called to tell me what had happened, I was shocked, concerned and panicked but also, I'm sorry to admit, annoyed. I hated being pulled into family shit, no matter what it was. My family felt like something I'd survived, something I'd escaped from. I only shared pain with those people, nothing else.

There are obligations, though, that you can't get past. I owed John. John had given me and Dave the money to go to Sydney, and he always knew enough about me to know that if I was going to etch out a decent life, it wasn't going to be in Auckland. Once when I was destitute in Sydney, I called John to tell him I was thinking about coming home. He just said, 'There's nothing for you here, Mark,' and hung up.

It wasn't just obligation and debt that made me want to go to John, though. I really wanted him to live, to survive.

I flew to Auckland after he got out of hospital and hung out with him in South Auckland for a bit. It was like old times: we played darts and talked a little bit about rugby, fighting and people from the neighbourhood. We hung out at the front of the South Auckland clubs, watching the nineteen-year-old versions of ourselves tumble drunkenly out of the doors and into street scraps.

John didn't have much to say to me and I didn't have much to say to him either, but I think me being there could have helped him. I don't know, maybe it didn't. He was broken, and I had no idea how to fix him. Seeing him like that brought the rage back in me. John was the second toughest bastard I'd known growing up (after our brother Steve), and a guy who was as good with his fists as me – maybe even better. Now sometimes talking to him was like talking to a fencepost. It wasn't right.

I left New Zealand angry with everyone in John's life, and also with John himself. Suicide was chicken shit stuff, I thought. That's not what men did. Men sorted their shit out. Men persevere.

I returned to Sydney despairing and angry, but also very happy to come home to Julie and the kids. I was thankful, too. John's vacant face would appear in my mind and I would think there but for the grace of God – and the grace of Julie – go I.

I wasn't built to look after my adult siblings. I was the baby of the family, man. Looking after my kids and my wife, that was my job. Beating the shit out of the other UFC heavyweights, that was my job.

After the Struve fight I was expecting to take a little break, but the UFC dished up an opportunity I just couldn't refuse. They asked me if I would like to fill in for the injured Alistair Overeem against the number-one heavyweight contender, Junior dos Santos, at the MGM Grand Garden Arena in Las Vegas. They only had to ask me once.

A former UFC champion, dos Santos had been the high-water mark in the UFC heavyweight division, having peeled off ten consecutive victories until his last fight, in which he lost a gruelling rematch against Cain Velasquez. Cain would also be fighting on that card, defending his title against Brazilian Antônio 'Bigfoot' Silva.

A win against JDS would almost certainly give me a shot at the winner of the title fight. I wouldn't have the luxury of a long camp, but I trained in Auckland and made plans to take my team to Vegas three and a half weeks out from the fight. I booked a house and a car, arranged a gym and got the boys and myself on a flight east.

When I turned up to the airport, though, it was a no-go.

'I'm sorry Mr Hunt, but we can't allow you to board that flight,' the Air New Zealand attendant said sweetly. I knew exactly what it was, too. It was the ghosts of drinking past fucking with me.

The incident took place on New Year's Eve in 2002, after I'd lackadaisically and unsuccessfully defended my K-1 title. I was on holiday in San Diego with Julie, hanging out with some Kiwi mates – roofers, fun lads who appreciated a drink and wouldn't shy from a scrap. We'd ended up at a lively beachside bar and the booze did flow – it was

New Year's Eve, after all. I was in a good mood. I was in California with my girl by my side and my mates . . . where were my mates?

I looked outside and saw the urgently moving crowd and shouts and shrieks of a fistfight. When I got there, it was all over. I tried to get back into the bar to find Julie and the lads, but when I got to the door of the bar, a cop stood in front of me and told me I couldn't go back in. I hadn't done anything but walk out and try to walk back in again. Sure, I was drunk, but no drunker than every other reveller out there, and Julie was inside.

'I just gotta get my girlfriend,' I told the cop as I tried to walk inside, but he stood in front of me and opened up an extendable baton.

'You're not going in, boy.'

Boy?

Maybe this prick was pissed off that he had to work on New Year's Eve, maybe he was just an asshole 365, but I didn't appreciate the threat. I walked up to him until we were toe-to-toe and asked him a question.

'What the fuck are you going to do with that baton?'

It turned out he wasn't going to do anything with it. Instead he maced me and called over to seven other officers, who jumped on top of me and sat on me. I thought about that moment when I saw the Eric Garner video. With mace in my face and seven dudes on my back, I couldn't breathe at all and there was no ref to come in and stop that shit.

I ended up being charged with disorderly conduct. I hadn't touched a soul, but that's just the way it works in the US. I paid the $5000 bail and got the next plane home.

Pride had been able to arrange my visa, albeit belatedly, for the fight against Butterbean, so I thought things would all be fine for that Vegas fight against JDS. Twice, however, my whole team went to Auckland airport in preparation for JDS, and twice we were told there was no point boarding our flight because I wasn't going to be let into the US.

I knew the UFC were making every effort to sort out my visa issue, but as time drew closer and closer to the fight, I was increasingly concerned. I was fairly confident I would get to fight – the UFC contributed pretty significantly to the coffers of the state of Nevada so they probably had quite a lot of political pull – but with every day I spent in Auckland things were going to be a little bit tougher out there in the Octagon against one of the best heavyweights around.

Four days before the fight I was told I was now free to head to the US. At that point I thought maybe it made more sense to fly a couple of days later and just stay on Auckland time, but I decided it would be best to get to the US as soon as I could – I didn't want to give Uncle Sam time to change his mind.

The fight was at the MGM Grand Garden Arena, part of a hotel complex that wasn't just the biggest in Las Vegas, but in the world. When I arrived there and saw my face up on the giant billboard on the Strip, a place that's usually reserved for blokes like David Copperfield, I filled up with pride.

I thought about the legendary battles that had taken place in this arena – Tyson versus Holyfield, De La Hoya versus Mayweather, Pacquiao versus Hatton, now Mark Hunt against Junior dos Santos. When Pride or K-1 came to Vegas they'd been a sideshow, but the UFC was the big show in Vegas, and fights at the MGM were the crème de la crème.

The surrealism reached its peak when I got to the fight and saw that Mike Tyson was in the crowd, there to watch. As a kid my wildest dreams would have included going to Vegas for one of Tyson's fights. Now here I was in Vegas, and not to watch him, but have him watch me.

I wasn't overawed as I walked to the ring, though. That's only happened to me once in my career – in my first K-1 fight against Le Banner. I was locked in and ready to go as I made that walk at the MGM.

Every other stress in the world disappears when I step onto that mat, and no other person in the world exists, except for the man I'm there to fight. John doesn't exist, nor does my old man. Not even Julie exists in that Octagon.

When I'm in that ring, I'm in church and God flows through me. I was born to be in that cage. In that cage, I'm free.

Junior dos Santos was up there with some of the best guys I'd ever faced. Often described as the best boxer in the division, JDS also had a pretty high-level BJJ black belt and the dude was quite a specimen of an athlete too – but he only had two arms and two legs.

When we were called to the middle for the instruction, JDS gave me the business stare. I gave it back to him. JDS and I got along well, but he was like me in that he knew how to turn on the switch when it was needed.

We touched gloves and it was on. After wheeling for the first ten seconds or so, I threw the first strike of the fight and it could be argued this was the moment I lost the fight. That's the thing about fighting. You only have to fuck up once, and you don't even really need to fuck up, you just have to have a little bad luck.

My first strike was a leg kick, trying to get into the meat of his thigh. My foot never got to his thigh, though, as my kick was intercepted by the hard bone of his knee. When I put my foot back down I could tell something had gone wrong but had no idea how bad the injury was until, later in the round, JDS dropped me to the canvas with the same arcing, overhand right he'd used to knock out Cain Velasquez.

When I was scrambling back to my feet I felt confused. I should have been able to get away from that long, looping punch, but it caught me plum on the scone. Why couldn't I move properly?

The first round was pretty close, but I would probably give it to him. When I got back to my corner I could feel a hot, throbbing sensation in my foot. I looked down at it, but one of my trainers had thrown a towel over it. They'd seen my right big toe, all weird and mangled, and had covered it up. Out of sight, out of mind.

In the second round it seemed I just couldn't get away from this big fucker. I'd see his jab coming, I'd move backwards . . . and then I'd still eat his fist. That happened over and over and over again. I couldn't get my fists on him, either – not with much power or in decent combinations. I'd push off my rear foot towards him but just wouldn't get any propulsion. It was like pressing a broken button on an old *Street Fighter 2* cabinet.

I managed to tag JDS a few times in the second and got a good combo on him against the cage, but he immediately shot in for a takedown. As soon as my back hit the ground the crowd started booing – it had been a decent scrap up to that point. The round ended with him throwing elbows from the top and as I went back to my corner, I knew I needed a KO in the third for the win.

By the third round I couldn't get any purchase from my back foot and had lost faith in my ability to pull any more good combinations together. When I saw an opening, I swung for a home run. JDS was too good for that stuff, though, so I just ate counter shot after counter shot after counter shot. I kept coming at him – I had no choice – until he slowed me with a heavy right, then finished me off with a spinning wheel kick that bounced off the top of my head.

When I realised where I was and that I'd been stopped, I was disheartened, but not crushed. Fair play, Cigano, fair play. I'll have to get your ass next time. Returning to the dressing rooms, I found that my toe was about as broken as a digit could be, not only sticking out at an obtuse angle, but with the bone piercing the skin.

The fight atop us in the card lasted less than a minute and a half, with Bigfoot being overwhelmed by Cain's volume punching. I really wanted to test myself against Cain – he was slowly revealing himself to be a generational talent up there with Fedor himself – but that privilege was now once again going to fall to JDS.

JDS and I were given the Fight of the Night honours. I was gutted that I hadn't won, but I was happy I'd come to this hallowed ground and added my own little bit of history.

After that performance, the UFC were going to give out another honour, one that in my estimation was second only to a title shot. I was going to headline a UFC event on my home soil. The fight was to be in Brisbane, against a man above me on the Las Vegas card. It wasn't the man I wanted, but it was a big scalp (literally) nonetheless, with Antônio Silva coming off a title shot, and considered right up there in the heavyweight division.

Before I got into training I went back to New Zealand for a wedding – Victoria's son Vinny was getting hitched. When I saw John at the wedding, I saw a man who was now completely absent. It was as though he was an NPC (Non-Playable Character) in the game of life – a zombie, with only a couple of lines of dialogue.

You'd be able to squeeze those few words out of John if he knew you, but if you didn't he gave you literally nothing. Julie tried to talk to him, but he had nothing to say to her. He managed to play with Noah a little bit, which filled us with hope, and also dread.

During that trip I started feeling strangely fearful that something might happen to our little ones. I wasn't concerned about John, but I grew deeply distrustful of the people around him. There wasn't anything that I could put my finger on, but I just didn't feel comfortable when any of them were with my kids.

Perhaps it was because I'd seen what could happen in South Auckland when little kids were left with fucked-up adults. Perhaps it was because I'd seen what could happen to a boy as strong and intelligent as John was, when their childhood is put in the hands of a monster.

I had happy, healthy Aussie kids and I just wanted to get away from Auckland, and take my kids with me. I wanted to take the kids home and get stuck back into my training.

I trained hard for that fight, and it's just as well, too, as the scrap against Bigfoot ended up being one of the most gruelling of my life. As an American Top Team fighter, I knew Bigfoot really well. Like a lot of the guys in the UFC's heavyweight division he's a good bloke, a kindly lion who only brings out the claws when it's necessary. Whenever he did bare his teeth, though, Bigfoot knew what he was doing. He had wins over Fedor, Overeem and Travis Browne. He'd lost twice to Cain, but that didn't mean much because everyone lost to Cain.

With a black belt in both judo and Brazilian *Jiu-Jitsu*, Bigfoot certainly knew how to fight on the ground, but he also liked to slug when he could. The dude has lunch-boxes for hands and, with my escapes and sprawls now well and truly on point, I suspected the decision would be rendered on the end of someone's fist.

The day of the fight, the crowd brought it, as the Aussie crowds always do. Being mates and teammates, I think neither of us really wanted this fight to be set, but when we got into the Octagon we were both ready to take the other out.

As the main-event fight this would be a five-round bout – the first of my career. It's likely both of us had that in mind when we started, as the first minute of the first round went by without any significant shots being thrown. Bigfoot managed to knock me down in the first round with a short right-hand shot, but apart from that punch I was the aggressor. The Brazilian's knockdown shot probably gave him the first round, though.

I started getting my hands going in the second round, aiming some good left and right shots through Bigfoot's gloves and into that ample jaw of his. He responded by repeatedly attacking my front leg. His first big leg kick was a minute into the round, and it landed behind my knee. There were a few more after that that I managed to shrug off until, with about half a minute left in the round, Bigfoot landed a kick on my shin that sent heat through my body – heat that felt similar to what I'd felt when Le Banner busted up my knee.

I switched my stance so he couldn't attack that leg anymore and managed to ride out the rest of the round, but when I went to my corner I thought my tibia was broken. Lolo advised me to avoid his leg kicks if I could.

With my leg busted I shot in for the takedown, which surprised and delighted the Brisbane Entertainment Centre crowd but probably didn't please my corner too much. Steve, especially, didn't like it when I deliberately took BJJ black belts onto the ground.

I got my right hand into Silva's face a couple of times in that round, with the second a heavy shot going straight down the pipe and into the Brazilian's jaw. Silva fell backwards like lumber. For a moment I waited, practically hearing Steve's voice in my head, but soon I was leaping into Silva's guard.

With my hips down and the Brazilian pressed up against the cage, I kept him on his back and dropped dozens of short, sharp punches and elbows until the horn sounded. The second round could have gone either way, but the third was definitely mine.

When I got back to the corner my right leg was still swelling up but having spent much of the round straddling Silva's body, it was feeling a little better. My right hand, though, felt numb and warm. I wondered if that was broken, too.

I took Bigfoot down at the beginning of the fourth and when we got back up I started throwing lead right elbows. I landed a couple and felt like Bigfoot was ready to go, so

I punched for a finish, swinging with exhausting combos. It turned out he was almost as durable as me.

After that exchange he came back at me and I ate a few shots that stunned me. Soon I was on the ground with Bigfoot in guard throwing punches and elbows. With 30 seconds left in the round things got even worse, when he took full mount, opened me up with some huge punches and tried for his own finish. I ended the round covered in my own blood, but he didn't get the finish. As the horn sounded, an exhausted Bigfoot was slumped over me.

When I finished the round I felt that heat in both hands. I had three possibly broken limbs, a cut-up face – my blond hair had turned to pink – and there was one more round to go.

When we got into the middle for the fifth, the crowd was roaring as Silva and I embraced.

Good stuff, mate. Now let's finish this thing.

I didn't know what the score was but I felt like I needed at least this final round to win. I started teeing off at Silva with punches, but I knew I couldn't keep it up – not only because I was exhausted, but because of my busted-up hands. So I started throwing more elbows. One landed, opening up a large cut on Silva's head, and then another. Soon claret covered half of his face.

Midway through the fifth, the ref paused the action so the fight doctor could have a look at the holes in Bigfoot's face, but that didn't bring a stoppage so we had to dredge up everything we had left, swinging until the final bell.

At the end every punter was on their feet; both of us were covered in blood and neither of us capable of even one more strike. We hugged at the end, not only because we'd shared something that won't quickly be forgotten, but also because I'm not sure either of us could stand up without the other's help.

As I recovered in my corner, Noah and Caleb both came down to see their dad. I was about as happy as a man could be. I still wanted the win badly, but I knew a loss wouldn't take away how special that fight had been. Regardless of the decision no one would be losing face, or esteem, in the eyes of Joe Silva, the UFC's main match-maker.

The first judge gave the fight to me, but the second and third called it a draw, rendering the decision a majority draw. When I got backstage, I found that the boss had appreciated the show.

This is the tweet Dana White sent as soon as the fight concluded:

'Both Hunt and Silva win FON [Fight of the Night] and both get their win bonus and I might buy them both

their own private ISLANDS!!!! Sickest HW fight ever!!!'
I'm still waiting on that island.

When I went to hospital, I found that I did have two
metacarpal breaks, requiring twelve screws, but both breaks
were in the same hand. I'd be on the shelf for a little while,
but not as long as I might have expected considering how
intense the fight had been. A couple of weeks into my
recovery I received a call from a journalist telling me that
Silva had failed his post-fight drug test, testing positive for
unnaturally high levels of testosterone. Our fight had been
turned from a majority draw to a no contest. It really didn't
bother me that much. I still got paid, it was one hell of a
scrap and it wouldn't hurt me at all in my title aspirations.

'Does that mean I get his bonus money?' I joked.

That journalist stitched me up, writing a piece suggesting
I'd lost respect for Bigfoot because of his use of testosterone
replacement therapy (TRT). For the record, I hadn't. Bigfoot
still had to get in that Octagon and eat my fists and knees.
It's not like TRT makes your nose any harder. That guy's a
warrior and, besides, I've fought a lot of guys taking much
more toxic shit than testosterone.

It would be eight months until I'd fight again, and while
I trained when I could, I spent a lot of time just hanging
out with the kids and Julie, going to church and living the
quiet life. I never thought it'd be the case but I found the

home life suited me. I've always been a fighter, even when I didn't think it would be my profession – it's always been how I define myself. In that break, though, I found I could also define myself as a dad and a husband.

I was happy when my next fight was arranged, though. I still had some momentum going in the heavyweight division and I felt like I was only a couple of fights away from a title shot. I would be headlining the UFC's third Japanese event, once again at my old stomping ground, the Saitama Super Arena. The man who would be sharing the Octagon with me was the one man in the UFC who made me look svelte, Roy Nelson.

Nicknamed 'Big Country', Nelson had a big gut, a mullet and a hillbilly-looking beard, and because of that he'd been underestimated for much of his career. Not anymore, though. Nelson had won *The Ultimate Fighter* reality show and had knocked out some of the best UFC heavyweights, including Nogueira, Kongo and my old mate Cro Cop. In his eleven-fight UFC career, all of Nelson's wins had come by way of knockout, and no one in the organisation had ever managed to knock him out. Not until I did, anyway.

It came in the second round, my uppercut. It was one of those punches where, as soon as it landed, I knew the dude was out. Roy had eaten a lot of big shots in the UFC and had always kept coming like a Terminator, but when that uppercut landed I knew there was no need to jump on him and keep doing damage.

I got Knockout of the Night honours and a few months later, at the World MMA Awards, Knockout of the Year honours – all divisions, all organisations. The honour I really wanted came a few weeks after that knockout. It was the honour I'd been fighting for since I came to the UFC. Hell, it was the reason I came to the UFC in the first place.

I'd been enjoying myself after the Nelson fight, expecting to have a few months off before getting back into the Octagon. When Dana called, it was only a few weeks after the Nelson fight, but I'd managed to pile on 22 kilograms above the heavyweight limit.

'Mark, I have an opportunity for you,' Dana said.

I knew then and there what it was.

'Who's out, Fab or Cain?'

'Cain. Are you in?'

Of course I was in. Shifting those twenty-plus kilograms would be a bit of a chore, but I would fight any man, any place, any time – especially for my first UFC strap.

Chapter 16

MEXICO CITY, MEXICO
2015

They don't get any more dangerous than Mark. You could be beating the crap out of him, but you always have to remember that you're only ever a second away from him knocking you out. You can never stop against him. Ever.

STIPE MIOČIĆ, UFC HEAVYWEIGHT

UFC 180 was the first-ever UFC event held in Mexico, with the main event announced as a heavyweight title fight between number-one contender Fabrício Werdum and Cain Velasquez, who was born and bred in the US, but as proud a man of Mexican heritage as you could find.

In Mexico, boxing rivals football as the country's most popular sport, so the UFC hoped they could tap into the nation's fight history. When the fight was announced, a season of the reality TV series *The Ultimate Fighter* (*The Ultimate Fighter: Latin America*) was commissioned by Televisa, Latin America's biggest TV channel, with Werdum and Velasquez as coaches and stars of the show.

The tickets went on sale and all the 21,000 seats in the Arena Ciudad de México were sold in the first eight hours of release. The scene was set for the organisation's most prominent fighter of Mexican descent to hold up the most valued belt in MMA in front of a packed home crowd.

Only it wasn't to be. As durable as he is in the Octagon, Velasquez has proved to be a highly injury-prone champion, sidelined a number of times in his career with various maladies. When Dana called, he explained that Cain was going to be on the shelf for some time, so the fight against Werdum would be for the UFC interim belt.

I knew moving all those kilos would be tough. Conditioning could also be an issue, with the fight happening at 2250 metres above sea level, a full 750 metres higher than Denver – where I first learnt about the tribulations of fighting at altitude.

I had three weeks to get ready to face one of the world's best ground fighters, who'd had months to prepare himself for the biggest fight in his career and had been at altitude for many weeks. Of course I said yes. When an opportunity like that presents itself, you say yes and then figure everything else out later. Win this fight, and I'd have not only some UFC gold, but a guarantee that I'd get to scrap with Cain sometime later on down the track. I wanted that badly. Cain is probably the best heavyweight MMA has ever seen, and I really wanted to see if I could knock him off his perch.

None of it was going to be easy, but it was do-able. After all, belt a bloke a couple of times properly and all the altitude training in the world won't stop you from going to sleep.

A couple of days later we were touching down in Mexico City, and when we got out of the airport there was some commotion, with apparently two groups of people there ready to pick us up. One group was with the UFC so we jumped in a car with them.

A few days later my manager got a call from the UFC rep saying there was a specific kidnap threat against me and Werdum, and that we should only leave the hotel when we absolutely had to, and even then it should be with armed guards. Steve also heard that the other group at the airport had been attempting to kidnap me.

I found out most of this information after the fight. Before the fight, I had enough on my plate – or not enough on my plate, as it were. It was a tough weight cut, that one. It just wouldn't fall off me, that extra weight, no matter how many calories I missed or how much I trained.

With the lack of food and very thin air I became a pretty grumpy bastard, and I wasn't the only one, as my corner had decided to eat as I did in solidarity.

Things got pretty testy between us until one day, when I decided we all needed a change of scenery and suggested we should get out of the city for a few days. We planned to drive south to Acapulco to jump into the ocean, see a little of the countryside and get some training sessions in away from the pollution of the capital.

Halfway to our destination we stopped at a roadblock, which was manned by a number of balaclava-clad men holding knives and machetes. As we approached them it became apparent these guys weren't police or army – they looked too young and small, and they weren't wearing uniforms. As it turned out, they were a student group fundraising.

The incident actually ended up being surprisingly chilled. The guys explained that they were protesting the killing of 42 student teachers in a town nearby, as well as the government's complicity in the murders, and they were trying to raise funds so they could support the victims' families. They were happy to let us go on after we gave them a very small contribution.

The trip was a good one, I suppose, but it didn't put any more food in my belly and my mood just got worse and worse right up until weigh-in. The situation was exacerbated by drama on the home front, with some keyboard warriors deciding to have a go at Julie, claiming they knew me and they had some compromising information on me.

It was something Julie and I sorted out easily when we were back together again, but thousands of kilometres away, and me near-delirious with hunger, it grew in my mind as something much larger than it actually was.

Even though that trip was the culmination of all I'd been working for since I got to the UFC, I was really missing Julie and the kids. I had wave after wave of melancholy while I was there, thinking a lot about my past and future, and my family, and my siblings back in New Zealand.

As I've said, I didn't think much about Steve, John and Vic when I didn't have to, but maybe my natural defence against unwanted thoughts was weakened by lack of food, or maybe the hunger was a mental trigger.

When I finally made weight and got to eat a decent meal, everything came back into focus. My team was a team again and I was a fighter again, but the thoughts of loss lingered. I walked into that Octagon ready to fight but, in the first round when I caught Werdum right on the chin and sent him onto his ass, I started to think about the life I'd built in Western Sydney.

I never usually thought about anything in the ring except the bloke in front of me, but in that moment, I thought about my kids and my wife. A pulse went through me, an urge to be with my wife and kids. It's a great impulse for a father and husband to have, but one that needs to be suppressed if you're also a fighter.

I took the first round of that fight, but I got knocked out in the second. It was a cleverly orchestrated move that did it, with Werdum faking a takedown and then launching into a flying knee. I was still ducking when it landed, trying to avoid the takedown that never came. It was a good knockout, that one. Clean. Well done, Fab, you got me good.

It was another fight I failed to win, but probably also another that didn't affect my stock in the division too much. I'd managed to knock Werdum down twice in the first round and had taken the fight on very short notice.

I still had at least three fights left with the UFC, and even after that loss I'd stay in the upper echelons of a division that didn't have too many big names excelling at the time. I figured I was still only one or two matches away from fighting for the belt.

It was still a very upsetting loss, though. I knew you only got so many chances at glory in the fight game – especially at the age of 40 – and regardless of the circumstances you have to seize your opportunities.

When I got home, any lingering disappointment over the fight disappeared as soon as I had Julie and my little ones in my arms again. I went back to sunny Sydney in spring, with days full of soccer practices, princess parties, toys and kids' meals. It was pretty hard to stay upset about the loss.

I only had a couple of weeks of sunny domestic bliss, though, until Victoria called and turned my world instantly cold. John was gone.

I couldn't believe it. Even though John had tried suicide before and was as vacant as he was when I saw him, I still couldn't believe he was dead. I still can't really believe it now. When I hung up the phone I waited for the wash of sadness to come, but it didn't. There was only shock.

I travelled back to New Zealand to help with the arrangements. John had left instructions for his body. In the church in which we'd grown up, it was essential that the body stays intact after death, but John had always hated that church and had insisted that he be cremated. John wanted out of this world, mind and body.

The service was at Mangere cemetery, just a couple of kilometres from where we grew up. It was a small ceremony, with just a handful of people, with my Sydney and Auckland families present, and a smattering of people from our childhood.

Of course it was a sad and sombre affair, but there was one moment I really appreciated. I didn't think it was in him, but Steve got up in front of everyone at the service and spoke about John and our father and what life was like when we were kids. Most people at the service were hearing about all that stuff for the first time.

I'm so proud of Steve for doing that and I'm also proud of Victoria for getting through all the trauma the way she did. I've never told them, and I probably won't, but maybe someone will read this and tell them.

I'm really thankful for the things John did for me, too. I might not have moved to Sydney without him, and without him I might not have stayed. I might not have fought in Japan without him. I might not have met Julie.

I wondered if there was something I could have said to John to keep him from doing what he did. I'm not sure I could have done anything. I never really got through to him, even when we were younger and it was considerably easier. I still wish I'd tried, though. In many ways John was a stranger to me his whole life, but maybe I could have helped him somehow.

If there is one message to take away from all this – this book, my story, my life – it would be that there's incredible power in talking to someone about the hurts happening in your life. Speaking to Julie in those early days changed my life like magic, as it did when I spoke to a counsellor in 2010.

I speak to God, too, and He is always there, always listening. With Him, I'm never alone, even when Julie and the kids aren't around. Without that, and without them I have no idea who I might be.

If you're depressed, speak to someone. Just do it. Just reach out. Hell, send me a message on Facebook if you want to, but whatever you do, don't keep it all to yourself.

I've never cried for John. I think about him all the time, but I can't really get into the sadness of it for some reason. I do honour his loss, though, by living my life in a way he never got the opportunity to.

Jules and I married in 2007, but it was a bit of a slapdash affair. We ended up tying the knot in the back garden of our place, after the boys and I had spent the night before partying at the Intercontinental Hotel. Maybe it wasn't the biggest and best wedding in history, but as far as I see it, a marriage is a marathon, not a sprint, and Jules and I have only just started to hit our stride.

The UFC wanted me to get back into the Octagon in a relatively short turnaround after the Werdum fight and I was more than happy to oblige. I'd only had one win over my previous four fights, but no one behind me had gained much contender momentum, either. When the rankings came out after the Werdum loss there were four guys in front of me: Cain and Fabrício, who were finally set to face off for the title; Junior dos Santos, who'd been beaten so badly in his last two title fights against Cain there was no appetite to give him another shot; and Croatian–American fighter Stipe Miočić. He'd only had two losses in his fourteen-fight career, with his last loss being a wafer-thin decision loss to JDS. When they scheduled me against Miočić in Adelaide, I couldn't have been happier. With the current status in the division, a win against Stipe could quite possibly mean a shot at Cain. It would also be a fight on home soil, and my fourth main event in a row. There was nothing bad about any of that.

After the Werdum fight my weight had started to balloon out again, but as I got back into my conditioning – and mostly thanks to Zuu training, a new type of intensive interval training that concentrates on primal, animal movements – I quickly started shedding the weight and getting my gas tank filled up again.

In the few months leading up to the Miočić fight I moved back to Auckland for my camp. My team of Steve and Lolo and conditioning trainer Alex Flint all lived in Auckland and I had great facilities and training partners there. An added benefit of being across the ditch was that I'd be away from my kids and all the delicious food that I liked to eat with them.

I trained hard during that camp and felt like I was getting where I needed to be, but I couldn't keep myself from flying back a number of times to hang out with the kids. I was working hard in Auckland, so when I was in Sydney I allowed myself some meals I probably shouldn't have had. I thought, *Fuck it, I've had enough kids' birthdays without any cake in my life.*

My weight was roughly where it should be a month before the fight – with fifteen or so kilograms to shed – but after that, I just couldn't seem to lose much more. When I flew to Adelaide a couple of weeks before the fight, I was still a good twelve kilograms over the limit.

The diet was strict in the house we were staying in, and the training relentless. Four days before the fight I went into the Adelaide Intercontinental to check myself on the official scales the UFC had set up in the basement of the hotel.

'Oh, that's not good,' I said to myself. I was still nine kilograms over.

Over those remaining few days my team did everything they could to help me shed my last kilograms. I trained and sweated and ate like a rabbit and, in the 48 hours before the weigh-in, we tried to strip all the water out of my body, first in a sweat suit and finally in a sauna suit. I started to cramp all over, with Steve having to punch my legs and arms regularly to keep them from locking up.

On the day of the weigh-in I still had quite a few kilos to lose. The cramping had moved to my jaw and I was delirious, speaking nonsense to a confused Steve and Lolo. I was in a starving, dehydrated daze. The boys thought it was time to admit defeat, time to get some food and water into me, and just go in heavy. There would be penalties for that, monetary penalties, and also a bollocking from Dana and the media, but my team didn't see that we were going to make it.

My jaw was still cramping up so it was hard to get any words out, but I made my thoughts on the matter clear. We were only a few hundred grams over, and I reckoned if we squeezed this stone just a little bit more, it felt like we could make it.

We got to the stadium with all the other fighters having already been on the scales, and just moments before I was supposed to get up onstage. The UFC was monumentally pissed with my team – they had requested that I turn up to the weigh-in hours earlier – but the television audience didn't know any better, so it was all fine. I got up on those scales and tipped them at 120 kilograms – the absolute limit for a UFC heavyweight fight.

At that stage of fight week I'm normally like a caged animal, but I was quiet and reserved after getting off the scales. In the post weigh-in interview I told Stipe he was getting knocked out but I didn't say it with much gusto, even though I did still believe it.

That night I invited everyone who had come to Adelaide to support me to the house for a barbecue. There were people from church, guys from Auckland and Sydney, my team, my training partners, Caleb and, of course, Julie. It was a big gathering, a long way from that first Sydney fight of mine deep on the toilet card.

Everyone was in good spirits that night. The stories rippled through the place about how close I'd come to not making weight, but that I'd managed to get under the bar with minutes to spare. I was happy, too, but in a restrained mood. For some reason I couldn't eat much, either, but got down what I could and headed off to bed with Julie nice and early.

I arrived at the ring feeling pretty good. I walked in to the song *Freaks*, made by a Samoan–Kiwi mate of mine, Savage and DJ Timmy Trumpet and as I got to the Octagon the crowd made it known why they'd bought their tickets. That stadium wanted a knockout, and I wanted to give it to them. One more knockout then I reckoned I was a good chance to fight Cain for the gold.

Stipe faced me in the middle of the Octagon, we touched gloves and started to wheel. After about twenty seconds he ran in, grabbed my front leg, turned me and dumped me on my back. I'd been slow seeing the shot and hadn't gathered nearly enough power pushing off him.

I knew in that moment my shitty weight cut had completely gouged my energy levels. There were 24 more minutes left to go in the fight and I was probably going to be getting a beating for most of them.

Chapter 17

SYDNEY, AUSTRALIA
2015

The scars are still there. For instance, I'm in charge of discipline with the kids because Mark's so terrified of overstepping that line. Also, if there are three of us eating, Mark will get enough for ten. He wants to make sure no one in his house will ever feel what he felt as a kid. He's become such a wonderful man. From where he started . . . it's pretty amazing.

JULIE HUNT

Stipe Miočić beat my ass like a *taiko* drum. I wasn't in that fight, not for a moment. I spent most of it on the ground eating punch after punch, and on the scant occasions that I did manage an escape and stood back up, Stipe would just pick my ass back up and dump me on the ground again.

I've never taken a beating like that in the ring. I'm not sure there are many people who ever have. It's no fun, being on the floor getting punched over and over again, but it's not that bad either. If things really turn to shit, the ref will stop it, and until then you're in with a chance. If you're still in a fight, things are never that bad.

I was ready to take that beating. I'm always ready, actually, any time I get in the ring. I'll never like it, especially if I end up losing, but if it goes down like that, then so be it. People starting out in MMA need to know that this isn't a game for those who aren't ready for the worst. You'd better not give a beating unless you're willing to take one too.

After that fight I was taken straight to hospital. While I didn't look too pretty, there wasn't any permanent damage. This big coconut head of mine isn't easy to crack.

Some people reckon Lolo should have thrown in the towel. Even more people think the ref should have stepped in much earlier than he did. All those people are wrong. I kept telling the ref I was fine, and Lolo knew that if he threw in the towel he and I were done.

It was just one of those things. I fucked up in that Miočić fight. I fucked up the weight cut and I went in to the fight weak and powerless. At the top of the tree it's a long way down to hard ground if you lose your grip like that.

I used to be able to just kind of roll into my fights. I used to be able to turn up fat or underprepared, knowing my fists would get me through. It's not like that anymore, though. The fight game's changed, and I've changed too.

I'm 41 years old. That's pretty old for a fighter. It's been 25 years since I first fought in the ring. When I think about that angry, wild dude in that first fight and look at the pages of this book, I can scarcely believe all that's happened to me. I never thought any of it would have been possible as a kid. I look at this book and I know I've lived a life. I look at these little smiling kids of mine, full of beans and happy, and I know it's been a good one.

I love being a dad and I love being a husband. Home is where my life happens now. I never thought I'd find a place where I could be more comfortable than in a ring, standing across from a man with his fists raised, but I'm slowly making my way to other people's version of normal life.

I've had the devil in me for a lot of my life. If he's in you, I reckon it's dangerous to say otherwise, and to that end, I've got him tattooed on my left shin. The devil is most dangerous when he's out of sight. He's a pickpocket like that. Catch him doing his work and ninety-nine times out of a hundred that old boy is running.

Some people can pretend the devil doesn't exist, and more power to them, but I've been in a room with the devil, standing large and in full form. I've seen what the devil's work can do, to both perpetrator and victim.

I have my God in me, too, tattooed on my other shin – the alpha and omega symbols – the beginning and the end of everything. God works completely differently from the devil. Call God's name and He goes to work; open yourself up to Him and He's with you. God's light has burned through the darkest days of my life. The church is fallible, yeah, but God? Never.

One side of me is good, the other evil. I know I've got both in me. There have been times in my life I've fought because of my left shin, and other times because of my right shin. Perhaps it's the conflict between the two that has brought me to where I am. That struggle to get closer to goodness has been my fire.

Noah started doing BJJ and *Muay Thai* this year. He's a natural athlete, that kid, but I don't know yet if he's a fighter. If he is a fighter, he's going to be a very different type from his old man. He's not going to have the struggle in him that I had, neither are my beautiful girls (Julie and I have had three now). That was guaranteed when those kids first met their wonderful mother.

It's taken four decades, but my struggle might be over soon, too. That'll probably nicely coincide with the end of my fighting career. I'll be surfing that wave right onto the beach.

When I do finish fighting, I'm not going to be one of those guys still in the gym, pounding protein shakes and beating up the twenty-something tough guys. When I'm done, I'm going to be *done*.

I'm going to be a dad. I'm going to eat what my kids eat. I'm going to be large, unfit and with a smile on my face that you can't budge with a jackhammer. Yeah, my days of making 120 kilograms are numbered.

I remember when I was a little kid I used to cry sometimes when Mum and Dad were out in the car eating their dinner, because that meant there wasn't any for us. Victoria would sometimes console me by telling me that one day there would be a time in my life when I would eat as much as I wanted, and different things every day. I couldn't quite believe her then, but I used to fantasise about her being right. Now I live that fantasy.

If my UFC career finishes because I can't make weight anymore, that'd be a happy ending. I still reckon I've got a few weight cuts left in me, though. I'll learn from that Adelaide fight. There's still some fight left in this old warhorse.

I just saw Fab beat up and then submit Cain in Mexico City. Things are pretty open at the top of the heavyweight division. He's the new champ, Fab – two for two at altitude. He beat me fair and square, but on another day . . .

I look at Werdum and I know I could take him out. It'd require a little work to get into the kind of shape I'd need to be in for one last run, but I feel like, at the end of the race, I still have a bit of a sprint in me.

People have counted me out before so there's no reason they wouldn't count me out now, but if the UFC sends me a bloke with two arms and two legs, I'll back myself.

I know I have a long, happy life ahead of me after fighting, so I reckon I'm good for a little bit more hard work, a little bit more pain.

I'm almost done, but not yet. Let's see what you've got for me, Dana.

Gummon.

Gummon.

Postscript

SYDNEY, AUSTRALIA
2017

The first edition of this book came out in November 2015, and I didn't know then it was going to mean as much as it does to me and to others. I'm not the kind of guy who talks about himself and his dirty laundry, and up until this book came out you could count on one hand the people who'd known the shit that had happened to me and my brothers and sister. Now tens of thousands of you know it all.

That would have been my worst nightmare a few years ago, people knowing about my dad, and Vic and Steve and John, and prison, and the drugs and all that shit. Now, after people have come and spoken to me and told me about them and their families and how they felt after reading the book, I'm proud that they know my story. I'm proud that people can see I stopped a pattern of family violence and abuse and that it is possible to move past bad times. Those memories were skeletons in my closet, but not anymore – I see things differently these days. Now, they're hurdles that I was eventually strong enough to get over.

I'm not a perfect man. I'm a sinner. I try, nowadays, to be better, though. That wasn't always the way.

Since the book, I reckon I've become a little easier to talk to. Before, I used to shut people down, especially people like Ariel Helwani and other journalists, sometimes because I was scared they were going to discover my past. Not anymore. It's all out there. No one can ambush me now.

The first edition of this book came out just before my rematch against Antônio 'Bigfoot' Silva at UFC 193. In some ways, this was the State of Victoria's thank you for changing some pretty stupid regulations. Previously, MMA was legal in the state but could only happen in a boxing ring, despite the fact that the octagon and cage are there for the safety of the fighters. The regulations were stopping the UFC from mounting any events there.

The Liberal state government was adamant that they were not going to reverse a ban on the cage, but Labor hinted that, should they come to power, maybe they would do something about it, and the UFC said, well, if that's the case then maybe we'd organise a big event at Etihad Stadium.

Labor won and the UFC did just that. UFC 193 would be one of the biggest events the UFC ever mounted, with Ronda Rousey, one of the biggest stars the sport has ever had, fighting another kickboxer-turned-mixed-martial-artist named Holly Holm. Earlier in the night I was booked to be banging against Antônio 'Bigfoot' Silva, the bloke I'd had a five-round war with in 2013, only to have him piss hot afterwards.

This was a big fight for me. Not only would I be fighting in front of 50,000 people, I was on a two-fight slide. Both losses were against the next two heavyweight champions, but they were still the first back-to-back losses I'd had since I was in that dark fuckin' hole of debt and disappointment.

I poured a lot into this fight. I did my camp in Thailand, at AKA, and got Mike Swick, a former UFC middleweight contender himself, to run things. I don't reckon I've ever come into a fight in better nick than that one. I certainly had less trouble with the weight cut.

As I'd said previously, I have no problem with Bigfoot as a bloke, but when I saw him I couldn't help but think about how debilitating my previous fight with him had been, and how much of that was due to the fact that he was on the juice. As I trained, I could still feel a sting in the hand that had been broken in that fight.

After our first fight, Bigfoot was flagged for having significantly elevated levels of testosterone and was banned from competing for nine months, with the ban coming into effect when the fight happened. Because of the injuries I sustained in that fight, Bigfoot got back in the octagon before I managed to. When I saw him for the media commitments and face offs and stuff for UFC 193, I couldn't stop thinking that he got a little slap on the wrist and I got broken bones. It was bullshit. If we were going to be on an even playing field, I was going to make sure that he was the one taking the licks.

Walking back into a stadium with fifty thousand people reminded me of the old Japanese days. But as the last, local fighter in a stadium full of Australians, the reception was much louder than anything I'd ever heard in the Tokyo Dome or Saitama.

There was a lot of interest in this fight, because the first time the two of us went toe-to-toe, there was a shitload of action. People were expecting more of the same but the fight ended up being a little bit of a fizzer.

Bigfoot looked like the same bloke as he'd been in the first fight but he wasn't. As we danced around, I could tell he was scared of me testing his chin out. I walked him around the cage, kicked his legs a little bit and then beat him into the cage and then into unconsciousness in pretty much our first serious engagement.

The crowd was roaring, but I couldn't help but be a little pissed off. As I looked up at the big screen, I saw the blow that had buckled the Brazilian's legs. It was a glancing punch that skimmed the top of his head. I could have belted him with that shot a dozen times in Brisbane and that juiced-up motherfucker would have kept coming at me. Now I saw the real Bigfoot, and his real chin.

It was hard to enjoy that win because I couldn't help but think about how I'd been cheated previously. Still, I had the win, I had no injuries, and it was a pleasure to be able to go to my after party with my boy Caleb and all the crew who'd helped me in camp in Thailand.

I decided to have a pretty quick turnaround after that fight. I didn't think that the Stipe fight was the proverbial cliff fall that a lot of people thought it was. I thought it was just a fuck up, and I had no doubt that I had one more climb up the mountain.

I was forty, but I still wanted that strap. This power in my hands was an element yet to be completely harnessed.

The UFC wanted me to headline a 'Fight Night' card in Brisbane next, against a bloke who had been top of the division, having held the strap and fought in five title fights – a dude by the name of Frank Mir.

Mir wasn't the anaconda-like grappling force that he had once been, but he was still a very dangerous opponent and in the top ten. Mir had been remade as a boxer, with two recent knock-out victories on his record, but I still thought his best chance would be on the ground.

Once again, it wasn't much of a test. Mir was happier to engage than Bigfoot, a number of times trying to grab onto my legs, and even sometimes being the aggressor in the stand up. Each time he came at me, though, I shrugged him off relatively easily and got a little bit more data on how his body moved. Then, in the third minute of the first round, I threw a little jab outside of his head, which I suspected would have Mir slipping to his right, and loaded up with a right hand to where I thought his slip would end.

I caught him just above the ear and, as he fell, I knew he was done. His eyes were still open, but there was nothing behind them.

And then it was announced that Frank Mir had pissed hot, too. He was caught using Turinabol, an anabolic steroid. This really fucking annoyed me. There'd been a big push in the UFC to clean the sport up. Or at least, they'd claimed there was. I'd had opponents take steroids before, but this one just incensed me.

I'd lived through the MMA steroid era, and I had the scars to show for it. Not only had my body been banged up, people had died and had serious injuries. I knew Gary Goodridge in that time, he was a good man. He'd had endless battles against steroid abusers, and now he's a shell of a man, memory shot to bits and needing help with most aspects of life.

The danger wasn't only facing the juicers. A month before my fight against Frank, I'd heard that former UFC champion and Pride favourite Kevin Randleman had died of a heart attack at age 44. Kevin never failed a drug test but, back when he was fighting, there were rarely tests to fail.

Things were supposed to be different now. The UFC was pushing to become a mainstream sport, like basketball and football, and if that was the case, it was supposed to be a level playing field for competitors, with athlete safety a major concern of the organisation.

But despite all the talk, I'd just fought another juicer. Mir never had a chance to get a hold on me, but I felt like I'd once again been exposed to a risk that was no longer supposed to exist.

Still, I had two wins under my belt, against two guys in the top ten, both first-round knock outs, and in the UFC heavyweight division that put me close to a title shot. Unlike some of the lighter divisions, there weren't young-buck shooting stars demanding to be recognised in the title picture, but refurbished fighters like me, who'd perhaps changed their fighting style or training and were still the most dangerous dudes in the division.

Fabrício Werdum, perhaps the most accomplished grappler in all of mixed martial arts, was letting his hands go more; Alistair Overeem was not the (almost certainly enhanced) wrecking ball that he once was, but was a cagey counter striker, choosing precision over power; and me, a guy who'd eaten donuts, smoked, gambled, and generally been a fat, lazy bastard from time to time, was acting a little more like a professional athlete.

I still felt I had gas in the tank, and also unrealised potential.

After the Mir fight, the UFC called asking me to sign another contract – a long contract. Dana White said that he wanted me to have the rest of my fights with him, and I didn't mind that. All the best heavyweights in the world were still in the UFC, and I was only a couple of punches away from the title.

My manager, Zen, started negotiations, and I was offered awesome money, a shitload more than almost all of the guys in the roster. But I was worth more than that. My worth is more impressive than my record. I can top a card in three continents. The UFC had to acknowledge that.

This contract was going to set me up, but I was still all about that title. I was given that gift, man, and I hadn't fully used it yet. I wasn't going to back down.

I got everything I wanted. But I was their guy now. A few weeks later, Dana sent word for me to stay ready and get my weight on point. I was likely getting a shot at one of the two big cards coming up, which were UFC 200, an upcoming mega-event; and UFC 205, the first event the UFC would have in New York after a ban on cage-fighting in New York State had been overturned.

I wanted New York – that event was going to be held at Madison Square Garden, and I loved the idea of South Auckland coming to Manhattan, but Dana told Zen it was more likely I was getting on that UFC 200 card.

I was having lunch with Ben, my co-author of this book, when Dana confirmed he wanted me for UFC 200. The event was only three months away, but it had no main event after Conor McGregor, a funny little bastard from Ireland who'd become a huge draw, argued with Dana and was pulled from the card.

Dana contacted me and asked if I was keen and able to fight at 200. I told him I wanted New York. He came back and said that he needed me for 200. 'Fine,' I told him. I'd be ready.

That was that. I was a worker, and I'd signed a contract. Boss needed me, I was there. It was only later that Ben asked who I was going to be fighting. I didn't know. When I hit Dana up he told me that that information would be revealed soon.

I started training, and shedding the extra kilos, working under the assumption that 200 was going to be my next scrap. Then the rumours started flying around – perhaps Brock Lesnar was coming back.

Lesnar had been the undisputed pay-per-view king of the sport before Ronda Rousey and McGregor came to the game. A giant ex-collegiate and WWE wrestler, the dude looked like a cross between a NASCAR fan and a giant condom stuffed full of ping-pong balls. He was the former heavyweight champ, but hadn't fought in the UFC since 2011.

The people around me were pretty excited about the prospect of me fighting this dude, but I wasn't that keen. Brock was unranked and I didn't think he'd get me any closer to that strap. I was gonna fight whoever they wanted me to fight, though. Mine is not to wonder why, mine is but to do or die.

The confirmation came a few weeks away from UFC 200. Ariel Helwani broke the news that Lesnar was confirmed for the event. A few days after that, Brock and Dana went on *SportCenter* and I was confirmed as his opponent.

I wanted to get over to Vegas as soon as possible – start camp, shed weight and get used to the conditions. I messaged Dana and told him this, and he said he was gonna help me out. This was very late notice for a fight so he wanted to make sure we were happy and ready to scrap.

He sent me the details of a place he'd arranged for me in Vegas. The place was a damn mansion, with a shitload of bathrooms and bedrooms, a huge pool, a games room – all kinds of luxury. I decided that I was going to bring some of the upcoming Aussie and Kiwi boys over for the whole camp. Not only could they help me train, but they could also see a little bit of what it looks like when you get to the top of the mountain.

They were hot, fun, useful days in Vegas. The weight cut wasn't easy, but it wasn't hard like it had been in Mexico City or Adelaide either. I felt good about the fight.

When fight week came along and I stood next to Lesnar I felt that something wasn't right. He seemed way bigger than me, and I was still a few kilograms over the heavyweight limit. My interactions with him and with Dana were a little odd, and everything felt, I don't know, unnatural.

There was a shitload of hype around UFC 200, and it became a circus when light heavyweight champ Jon Jones got pulled from the card. There was a mad scramble to get contender Daniel Cormier an opponent. There were rumours floating around that the UFC was about to be sold, and there was a shitload of promotion all across the US and global media.

It was pandemonium. I just had my head down and my bum up getting ready for that big vanilla gorilla. None of the drama had anything to do with me.

I was confident of smacking Lesnar's lips and putting him to sleep, but the fight didn't go that way. He took me to the ground more easily than anyone I've fought before. I couldn't believe his strength. He'd shoot in for a take-down and I'd be sure that I'd be able to shrug him off, but before I knew it I'd be going for a ride onto the floor. There he'd just lay on me, sometimes posturing up for tiny little rabbit punches.

When the bell sounded at the end of the third round, I was pretty dismayed. That was no fucking fight. When they called out Lesnar's name, I clapped. It was no fight, but he beat me, fair and square. He used what he had, which was an almost unnatural amount of strength, to get me off balance and on the ground, where I was swimming, to get the win. Can't hate on that. Or so I thought.

Turned out it was an unnatural amount of strength.

There's quite a bit that I can't talk about here, as I'm currently suing the UFC but the indisputable facts of the matter are:

- That big pale fucker failed not only his post-fight, but also pre-fight drug tests.
- Lesnar was given an exemption for drug testing, and didn't have to take as many tests as a returning fighter should.
- The UFC was sold a few days after UFC 200 for more than US$4 billion.
- Lesnar made many, many millions of bucks from that fight, and very little of it was forfeited for cheating.
- I could have been seriously hurt because of that flat-topped fuckhead's cheating.

What's in question is whether the UFC suspected that Lesnar was on the juice, and whether they did everything they could to make sure it was a clean fight.

Others may not see it this way but I don't reckon the UFC did everything they should have to make it a fair fight. Brock and the UFC all came out pretty much unscathed from this whole thing. The UFC got to save a marquee event. The company was sold for billions. Brock took a pay cheque, and went back to the WWE without getting his lips smacked off. The only person who suffered was my black ass.

I wasn't injured, but I could have been. My loss was overturned into a no contest, but the fans don't give a shit about that. The result sent me quite a few steps back from the title.

I know I was expected to fuck off back to Sydney, shut up, and just get ready for my next fight against some steroid-abusing egg. I've shrugged my shoulders and moved on before, but not this time.

I'm not the same man I was in the K-1 and Pride days, and the sport has moved on too. This is a multi-billion-dollar sport now. With Hendo leaving, I'm the oldest fighter in the UFC. Things have changed, and if I didn't kick up a stink about this bullshit, then who would? Someone had to say something.

When I got back to Sydney I couldn't stop thinking about how my kids and Julie could have been affected if I got injured in that fight. I was on the shelf for a long time after that first Bigfoot fight, and Brock could have done even worse to me. Who pays for my mortgage if that happens? Who pays for groceries?

I thought about the young blokes I was training with in Vegas. I came up in a tumble, falling into a sport that wasn't even really a sport at the time, it was run by gangsters, shysters and opportunists, but things had changed. The sport is worth billions now, so surely we should get out of the fucking shadows. If one of these young blokes who trained with me in Vegas is the best in a fight, then he should win, not some juiced-up asshole. This is fucking fighting, not *Bold and the Beautiful*.

'Fight the fights on your contract, take the money, shut the fuck up.' That's what a lot of people wanted me to do. The UFC wanted that, and even a lot of my fans did too. I just couldn't.

The UFC kept offering me fights. They offered me JDS in Toronto and Barnett in Melbourne. I turned them both down. Just as well I didn't take the latter as Barnett is currently on the shelf after the US Anti-Doping Agency (USADA) informed the UFC of a potential anti-doping policy violation.

I would have loved to have banged with JDS again, though – I'm always down to avenge a loss. I would have loved to have thrown down with Anthony 'Rumble' Johnson too, who I was offered when UFC 208 lost its headliners Max Holloway and Jose Aldo. They were trying to save the card. Normally, I'm your man. Normally, standing and banging with Rumble in New York would have been the ultimate. Normally. Not this time.

Drug cheats are a pebble in my shoe, a bee in my freaking bonnet. I needed to do something. I thought about it all the time, about how nothing ever changes. The UFC are supposed to look after their athletes, but it seemed to me they're just like every other fucker, shaking my hand while their other hand is in my pocket.

With people like this, money talks. I spoke to my lawyers about a lawsuit around UFC 200 and they were into it.

Like I said, I can't say too much about the legal ins and outs of this thing, but I can say, it feels right.

•

While all that legal shit was going on my mum died. My sister called to tell me that it had happened, and I was relieved. It's good that she's dead. I don't say this from a place of spite, I say it because it's what was best for her. Her mind was there but her body was gone and I'm sure she was stuck in a torturous prison of her own memories. Better dead than that.

I was at home when I got the call and all I thought was, 'Okay, I'll pay for the funeral and then that's that.' I had no emotion left for her. Not fear, not anger, not pity, not anything. She was dead in my mind, and now her body had followed.

Last time I met with my mum I sat with her and told her I'd forgiven her, but maybe I did that for me, not for her. I still had a lot of anger when I thought about her. She never helped my sister. It would have been hard for her to help, but mothers are meant to do what's hard. Julie does whatever our kids need. Me too. My mum let it all happen.

I visited her in the home she was in, and although she couldn't move or talk because of the strokes, I could tell that she was trying to tell me something. She had to get something out. She was scared. She knew she was going somewhere and she was terrified about that journey. She had to say something to me, maybe that would make the journey easier.

But it was too late. I prayed for her, went home and knew I would only see her one more time, at her funeral. When I did see her, I felt love, but not for her, it was for my little ones and for Julie. When I left my house in South Auckland as a troubled kid I gave myself permission to be on my own, to walk away from anything I was attached to at the drop of a hat. I was a unit of one.

All that changed when I met Julie. Whatever happens, I'm never going to be on my own again. I am always going to be a dad to my kids. There's no circumstance in which I'd walk away from them. There's nothing I wouldn't do for them.

That's love, man.

•

Eventually I had to take a fight or else I was going to be in breach of contract.

I wanted the money for Julie and for my kids, too. I didn't feel like helping out the UFC, but I wanted to take their cash so I could prepare for when it all stopped. My contract was good, and I started thinking about my end game.

The UFC wanted me to take on Alistair Overeem. He's someone who's had speculation over a failed drug test hanging over his head for years, but it's not really like I had a choice so I said I'd do it – UFC 209, Las Vegas, March 2017.

My lawyer filed a civil suit against the UFC, Dana and Brock Lesnar a couple of days after the UFC announced my fight with Overeem. When I got to Vegas, all anyone wanted to talk about was the lawsuit and steroids, and I was happy to oblige them. This was the fight I was in, more than anything else, so in many ways it seemed appropriate.

Camp was tough. I still think about that gift and that strap, which gets me up in the morning and agreeing to those extra rounds. But as the oldest dude in the entire 500-fighter roster, I can't pretend like I do it easy.

Overeem knocked me out cold. It was a tight fight until then, but in the third he caught me with a knee in the clinch, and that was that. I'm not saying I lost because I was concerned more with this lawsuit than the man across from me in the octagon, but I'm saying that, near the end of my career, I have different priorities in life now. That fact doesn't make me sad, it makes me proud.

It hasn't been an easy career and it hasn't been an easy life, but when it was time to fight, I fought. I didn't always prevail, but I always fought. The fight was in me. I haven't given up on the possibility of grabbing that belt, but I won't be tortured if I never get it.

I may train other people when I'm done. I may never go into a gym again. You may never hear from me again. I'm not sure yet. I want my story to end soon with a 'happily ever after' that involves a big, comfy chair, video games, some happy kids and lots of delicious food. No more fights, in or out of the octagon. I know now I fought because I had to. Soon I may not have to anymore. That's a good thing.

I understand fighting now, in and out of the octagon, and although I'm not much for speeches, I gave one the day before I fought Overeem. The NZ rugby sevens team was in town and they wanted to present a jersey to me in their hotel room. That was cool. The coach asked if I wanted to give a short speech. Normally I would have said, 'nah, I'm sweet,' but seeing that they were all young, eager blokes, there was something I wanted to say.

This is something I want to say to you, too.

It's a quote from Teddy Roosevelt, who I know absolutely nothing about except that he knows his shit. It goes like this:

It is not the critic who counts; not the man who points out how the strong man stumbles, or where the doer of deeds could have done them better. The credit belongs to the man who is actually in the arena, whose face is marred by dust and sweat and blood; who strives valiantly; who errs, who comes short again and again, because there is no effort without error and shortcoming; but who does actually strive to do the deeds; who knows great enthusiasms, the great devotions; who spends himself in a worthy cause; who at the best knows in the end the triumph of high achievement, and who at the worst, if he fails, at least fails while daring greatly, so that his place shall never be with those cold and timid souls who neither know victory nor defeat.

This is a quote about life, not sport. I'm not going to be the man in the sporting arena much longer, but once you've dared greatly in one arena, I see no reason that you can't dare again in another. And whatever I'm doing, I know now that it's all about the endeavor, not what some peanut on the internet is saying about how you're doing it.

The lessons I've learned fighting will be the wisdom I use to raise my kids, love my wife, worship my God, and live the rest of this life, which hopefully will be long and peaceful, and maybe with that UFC belt in the lounge room.

Hey man, you read the book. Stranger things have happened.

INDEX

If you would like to find out more about Mark Hunt you can follow him on Facebook or Twitter:

Twitter.com/markhunt1974
Facebook.com/therealmarkhunt

You can also check out Mark's Juggernaut apparel and fight gear on Facebook or the website:

www.jugnt.com

APPAREL & FIGHT GEAR BY MARK HUNT

If you are struggling with depression, anxiety, gambling addiction, grief or abuse, or just need someone to talk to, here are some contact details that may assist you.

Helplines

Mind: 0300 123 3393 or text 86463 with a question.
Sane: 0845 767 8000
Samaritans: 116 123

Resources

www.mind.org.uk
www.sane.co.uk
www.samaritans.org
Beyond Blue: http://www.beyondblue.org.au
The Black Dog Institute: http://blackdoginstitute.org.au
Headspace: http://www.headspace.org.au